CENTER
MONOLOGUES
FOR WOMEN

TE DUE

THE PLAYWRIGHTS' CENTER MONOLOGUES

FOR

WOMEN

EDITED BY KRISTEN GANDROW
AND POLLY K. CARL

HEINEMANN
Portsmouth, NH

Heinemann
A division of Reed Elsevier Inc.
361 Hanover Street
Portsmouth, NH 03801–3912
www.heinemanndrama.com

Offices and agents throughout the world

Performance rights information can be found on pages 207–8.

Library of Congress Cataloging-in-Publication Data
The Playwrights' Center monologues for women / edited by Kristen Gandrow and Polly K. Carl.
   p. m.
  ISBN 0-325-00741-1 (alk. paper)
  1. Monologues. 2. Acting—Auditions. 3. Women—Drama.
4. American drama—20th century. I. Gandrow, Kristen. II. Carl, Polly K.
III. Playwrights' Center (Minneapolis, Minn.)
  PN2080.P6215 2005
  812'.045089287'09045—dc22   2004025908

Editor: Lisa A. Barnett
Production: Elizabeth Valway
Typesetter: Kim Arney Mulcahy
Cover design: Jenny Jensen Greenleaf
Manufacturing: Louise Richardson

Printed in the United States of America on acid-free paper
09 08 07 06 05 VP 1 2 3 4 5

To Barbara Field, John Olive, Tom Dunn, Erik Brogger,
and Jon Jackoway, the founders of the Playwrights' Center.
What a great idea!

Contents

Creating the Life of Theater

The Playwrights' Center in Minneapolis is celebrated by emerging and established playwrights as an essential artistic home. We nurture artistic excellence and new visions of theater, foster playwright initiative, and advocate for playwrights and their work. We continue to develop a community for new work in the American theater.

The genesis of new plays is with playwrights—and monologues—like those represented here. This collection showcases the spectrum of writing for the theater that is crafted by Playwrights' Center members.

Within these pages you'll find a mother's introduction of her twenty children, murderers and adulterers, and a survivor from a boat lost at sea who can now contemplate the future. There are women of a certain age coping with architecture gone awry, sexuality, loss and death, independence and war. You'll enjoy the intelligence and subtlety of a young woman leaving her boyfriend, a girl whose trailer-park world is disappearing, and a woman describing her first experience with death. You'll engage with girls and women escaping from violence and disability, handling affairs or aging, and explaining themselves to a world that seems to misunderstand. The characters in these striking monologues embrace life, learn to accept death, and live fully everything in between.

Playwrights write for *live* theater, for actors in front of an audience. These monologues feature outstanding writing for actors to seize, speak from the heart, and bring the words' actions to life for us. These are the words playwrights create and need to hear "in the actors' mouths." The monologues in these pages are artistic tools for actors that allow hilarious, poignant, passionate, and spirited interpretation. When performed for acting classes and auditions, these monologues virtually guarantee unique material—a bonus for everyone involved.

New plays—and especially monologues like these—provide us with a powerful collective experience. In the theater with other people, strangers and artists alike, we share a space where new worlds are imagined and the complex issues of our lives are examined.

The aesthetically diverse voices of Playwrights' Center members speak with conviction, honesty, and humor. A collection of our playwrights' monologues for men is available in a companion volume. This set of books belongs on the shelves of every actor, theater educator, and playwright. We hope you'll agree!

—Kristen Gandrow

A Destination for Playwrights

The Playwrights' Center in Minneapolis has been developing new plays for the stage for nearly thirty-five years. During that time we have had the opportunity to work with some of the most important American playwrights, including August Wilson, Mac Wellman, Naomi Wallace, Lee Breuer, Craig Lucas, Theodora Skipitares, Suzan-Lori Parks, and Jeffrey Hatcher, to name a few. Plays by our writers have won every major award in the American theater.

Our presence as a vital new play development center is thriving, and our impact is reaching ever further, to playwrights at every level of their careers. The center annually awards more than two hundred thousand dollars in fellowships and grants. We are a national membership organization with more than four hundred members across the United States—some writing their first plays and others winning their first Obie award. The center is a creative home where playwrights can explore writing for the theater, emerge as new dramatic voices beginning to be heard throughout the country, and sustain professional careers as dramatists. The vital and engaging environment at the center offers playwrights encouragement and the creative freedom to imagine theater in every shape and genre.

The center's programs provide many varied opportunities for playwrights. Every Wednesday night at our roundtable, Twin Cities professional actors volunteer to read a new play, and a playwright-filled audience offers feedback and answers questions from the evening's featured playwright. Additionally, our playwrights' lab brings collaborators together throughout the year for workshops and readings. Each year, produced plays throughout the country have their start at the center—as a seed of an idea or exercise in a playwriting class, a cold reading of a first draft, a staged reading, or a workshop.

We recently awarded a Playwrights' Center McKnight Residency and Commission to Craig Lucas. His development process at the center encapsulates our strength in bringing new plays to the American stage. Craig started with a proposal, which led to a first draft. Joined by some very talented local actors and a director from New York who is familiar with Craig's work, we spent an intense dramaturgical month workshopping the play with all of the collaborators. Rehearsals began two months later, and we launched a modest production. One year later, *Small Tragedy* won the Obie award for best new American play after moving from the Playwrights' Center to an Off-Broadway stage. Craig said of his time at the center, "I've never had a better experience developing a new play anywhere, in any venue, in this country or elsewhere."

Our members are the heart of the organization. The stories of the center's impact on playwrights' lives are myriad. Melanie Marnich tells of living in Cincinnati, working in an advertising agency, and becoming a member of the Playwrights' Center before she ever wrote a play. She knew she would eventually make her way to the stage, and regular communication with an organization for playwrights provided exactly the inspiration she needed. Since becoming a member, she has won numerous fellowships through the center, including a Jerome in 1999 and 2000 and a McKnight Advancement Grant in 2001 and 2004. Melanie's plays have won multiple awards and have been produced around the country, including twice at the Humana Festival and Off-Broadway.

Lee Blessing has said, "Without the Playwrights' Center, I never would have been a playwright." Referring to the center's pluralism, Blessing said he considers the center "one of the most important opportunities in the entire field of the arts." Our openness to new voices and new forms creates a palpable energy that spreads across the nation and infiltrates theaters around the country. It's impossible to see new plays without encountering the center's impact on the field.

—Polly K. Carl

To Stay or to Go Blues

JANET ALLARD

A spotlight on a porcelain coffee mug of fine design. She speaks.

You staying or going? To stay or to go?

Go ahead, make up your mind, make my day. Stay. Eyeing those paper cups, asking what a tall is? What do you think this is, you half-class half-ass lack of sophistication stuffed shirt, think this is a McDonald's? Think this is a fast food to go kind of place? You're sipping something fine, hon, shade grown. Why not stay awhile? Why not sink into that chair and pretend you're not in a chain restaurant, but in a fine place with fine music, not marketed for your enjoyment, but played by a band.

To stay then, right? C'mon, make up your mind. What's a matter, afraid of commitment? You're a stayer. I applaud commitment. You're a stayer. We have that in common. We'll get along fine. I knew you were a stayer from the minute I laid eyes on you, not afraid of commitment, not a man who shrinks from commitment.

Sit with me, doll, anywhere. I like the couch, personally. Let's get cozy.

Sugar. Yeah, sugar, I like sugar. Some sugar. You like sugar, you like a lot of sugar, hold on honey, that's getting sweet, easy, easy. Too much sugar can kill a thing.

How 'bout a first sip, babe, I'm not that hot. Won't scald you, I promise. Just a little test, you don't have to use your tongue, just your lips. Don't blow babe, that's not becoming.

No one stays anymore.

You're different.

No one takes the time to hold my handle, warm their hands around my sides.

They take it in a paper cup and they're out the door. Not you, you're a sensualist. You take your time.

What you got there? The crossword. Who's that guy across from you? Suit and tie. Looks like a starched shirt. That your boss? Give him a sip of me, go ahead. He's looking at me. It's different when it's to go, it's a quickie, it's sloppy, it spills on your coat. You got to take the time, hold me in your hands, feel the curve of me against your lip. You're getting sharp now, you're getting witty, full of ideas, you got brilliant bright ideas, you think fast, you're a do-er, a man of action, you're the main attraction, you're on fire. Just the way I like you. A six-letter word for cow. Bovine. Now you're cooking. Could it be I've got something to do with it? Naw, I won't take the credit, hon, drink up, gulp me down. I'm here for you. We're a nation of do-ers. Of excited, motivated people. Beginning with me and you, you and me. I speed you up, make you fast. Without me, you'd work a lot less, hotcakes, and where would we end up? A nation of unmotivated, unworking people, relaxing like jelly on their sofas, lounging. Where would that leave your country, pal? Without you? Without me? In a rut.

You like that music, tapping your foot, movin' your leg, you got nice legs.

You're all excited.

"You Got Me a Buzz"
Don't know where this feeling's coming from
But I ain't like I was
I got something spinning, pulsing through my blood
I'm on fire, in love, on fire.

Hey. Who's that?
She your daughter? Your girl? You didn't tell me.

Thought this was just me and you. Didn't know you invited someone to join us. If you don't watch it, you're gonna make me jealous.

Go ahead, sit down, sister. Take a sip of me. Why not pretend you're sophisticated, in sync, not sunk, in sync, in the groove, in the flow. That's right, you're getting excited now, I can see it in your lips. You're starting to shake a little, baby. What is this, your first cup? Thought you were a pro? You're not even sixteen are you? You're a baby, coulda fooled me with that lipstick ring around my porcelain, thought you were a pro. How'd you end up with this guy?

What do you mean I'm getting cold? Of course I'm getting cold, you haven't touched me in minutes. Why'd you tell her I was cold? You're running your mouth off, of course I'm getting cold. You would, too. You would, too, if someone ignored you for this length of time, yammering away like I'm not even right here in front of you. And she's an amateur. Listen, sister, you're getting to be a bore. Ho hum. Time's a tickin'. I'm losin' my buzz for you both.

"You Got a Headache"
I'm turning lukewarm
Don't know how long we been here
But you're losing your charm
Get on the road now, just walk out that door
I won't cry for too long, I won't be too blue
Just know that when you're gone
Someone else can sip me, too
Before you go be sure you're sure
Don't slam the door, behind you is
Another consumer.
I ain't gonna miss you honey
You're just like the one before
I won't call or try to find you, I won't stare out the window for you
When it comes to commitment sippin', you haven't got a clue

You can be assured, there's another Joe behind you
He'll stay with me and treat me fine, and look into my porceline.

When you walk out that door, there'll be another one behind you.

Another just like you, with better taste.

I'll be fine. There's a line out the door. They're waiting for me. You better get moving with those big ideas of yours. Go ahead, no hard feelings.

To stay is temporary, anyway.

We all know that.

Just remember your cinnamon girl. Come back tomorrow. Same place, same time. A little class, a little milk. A little froth. A little grace. I'm your cinnamon girl.

Don't forget this feeling. The excitement. Come back tomorrow and ask for me.

You just gonna leave me here on the table? Looking after you as you walk out that door?

Give me a last sip.

Good. Now go to work.

Night Time

JANET ALLARD

A Chinese woman from a mythical world, floats, stranded in the middle of the sea, searching for her husband.

MENG JIANG: I floating, but no can sleep, Mr. Jiang. I tip my head back to catch rain in my mouth just like you and me in the field when we married long time ago. I wait for ghosts all night. You know about me out here all alone all night Mr. Jiang? You know about me, right?

(Mr. Jiang's coughing can be heard.)

Mr. Jiang? Mr. Jiang? I hear you coughing. Is that you, is that you coughing? I brought you some good herb candy for your throat. Is something caught? In your throat? Speak to me.

(More coughing, Mr. Jiang comes into view. A distant figure. He tries to clear his throat to speak.)

Something caught?

Here. Candy. You like, remember, good for you so you no stay awake all night, remember?

I can hear you, I can hear you all right. I hear you fine. Talk to me.

Of course I hear fine. You like this dress, I always wear it, the same one.

What's wrong? You don't know me?

Mr. Jiang, of course it's me it's me it's me it's me. You and me, we went to Minnesota and had two babies, and we had to drive all across the top of America and come in the side so they wouldn't catch us and we settle down together you and me, you remember?

How come you never came to me? Since you've been dead? How come you let it all go flush, straight down the toilet, out, bye bye never see you again.

But now you're here. Here you are.

Maybe you can stay a little while, I have a very comfortable place for you to sleep, right next door to me. Right beside.

What's wrong, you don't know me? It's me. It's me.

I'm the same girl.

Maybe before, I look different.

Maybe you can stay, I made soup in the stone bowl.

Where is it?

Maybe I dream about that. Maybe I wanted you so much I dreamed I made you soup and then you came.

You were so clever, Mr. Jiang, so smart. Remember you told me the story, you told me the Emperor told you, "Use the bricks and build a wall as far as you can see and as many miles high and over our heads so that when I die my soul will try to go up. No can. Try to go to the side, no can, try to go and go and go. No can. And so it will come back to me and I will live as Emperor forever."

And tell me what you did Mr. Jiang, tell me tell me tell me.

But you built the wall with yellow porous bricks, millions of tiny little holes. Millions of tiny tiny little holes.

(Mr. Jiang is farther away.)

You can stay a little while.

Not time for work.

(Mr. Jiang becomes background.)

No.

(Mr. Jiang makes a motion to speak but cannot be heard.)

What? No. You stay. You stay and talk. You hold my hand.

(Mr. Jiang raises his hand, moves farther and farther beyond until he cannot be seen, his presence no longer felt.)

Bye bye, for now. Bye bye. Mr. Jiang I still hoping. Mr. Jiang I still hoping there is more and more and more. One day you gonna come back and find me the best little girl grown up then, grown all the way up then, old lady then, everytime you see me you think I change. Not quite sure who I am every time, every time you think your ghost end up in the wrong place.

Visit the wrong little girl. Still me Mr. Jiang, still me inside her, this wrinkle lady. I still hope there is more in store for you and me to do.

(Silence)

May be? May be huh?

(Silence)

Bye bye Mr. Jiang. May be huh?

Anne Yoshimoto

JANET ALLARD

A Japanese woman in her thirties. December 8, 1942. Honolulu.

ANNE: Sam Yoshimoto. Five-foot-six. Thirty-five years of age. Last seen wearing a brown dock worker's uniform. Last seen Pearl Harbor. 8 A.M. Yesterday.
(She holds up a photograph.)
This is my husband. Have you seen him? Are you okay? You look a little shaken up, me too. Are you okay?

My husband, he say, "I'm going to work." I haven't seen his face in two days. My husband, he say, "I'm so glad we came to Hawaii, so beautiful here, you so lucky you were born here." He is from Japan. I teach him to talk better English from Mother Goose. He learn with our kids. Chicken Licken, the sky is falling, fee fi fo fum, the sky is falling.

Yesterday. He wake up early. He say, "I'm going to work." Why do you go so early? Come back to bed, I say, come stay, warm in here, it's chilly out there. "I'm up," he say. What you going to do so early. "I going shoot the shit," he say, he pick up all the boys' talk like a toilet at the docks. Pearl Harbor.

Have you seen him? Look close. I hear nothing. Two days now.

Mochico. Her husband call. Right after. He's busy working, cutting into the Oklahoma, the damn thing is sunk with thirty-two men still inside, they trying to use the torch but the damn thing would blow up, so they cutting through the metal by hand. "The water is on fire," he say. Thirty-two men still inside.

Do you ever feel useless? I'm a teacher. But today I wish I was a nurse.

I can see the harbor from my window. All the lights off. They say. So I keep my lights off. Sherri's son, he call, he say, "I

8

seen the planes coming with the red meatball on the wing," he say, "I seen the guy's face, the pilot, so close I could hit him with a rock if I had a rock, so close so CLOSE I could see his expression. He was smiling."

When I look in the mirror this morning I notice I'm Japanese. What am I supposed to do? I'm Japanese. On the radio, they say Japan is the enemy. Is that what you see when you look at me? Is my face different today than it was yesterday? What do you think? Are you different today?

Where is Sam? Is he here? Someone said they took him for questioning. Took him where? I come down here to ask you. Maybe you would know.

Here. I brought you some *mochi*. Would you like to try? You know, *mochi*? Rice flower, sweet, pink, white, blue, green? It's Sam's favorite. Is he here?

My name, you can write this down. Is Anne Yoshimoto. My husband is Sam Yoshimoto. He is five-foot-six. Black hair. Brown eyes. He is Japanese.

Is there anything you can tell me? Ask me? I'm here to cooperate. We are all in this together.

All the other wives, they sit and wait. I cannot sit. I cannot wait. They say I'm in danger to come see you, to take the bus, because outside rumors are flying like fire and people are trigger happy today if you're Japanese. I need to do something, anything.

From your window you can see, the sky is smoke. Does the smell stay in your nose, all day, all night. Do you wake up and smell burning, burning oil, burning skin? Where is Sam?

Do you have questions for me? Would you like to know what I think of Japan? When I was last there? Who I know? Who comes to visit? Can I sing "The Star Spangled Banner"? Do I love my country? Yes. And your eyes say, "Which one?"

How do you tell a little girl her father can't come home tonight? Why? Because he's being held for questions. Why? Because he's Japanese. Why? Because he works at Pearl Harbor

9

maintenance. Why? Because Pearl Harbor on fire. Why? Because Japan hates America? Why why why?

But am I Japanese? Yes. But am I American? Yes.

My son he say, "Mommy am I a Jap?" Japanese. He say, "Am I Japanese?" I say Yes. He say, "Did the Japanese bomb Pearl Harbor?" I say Yes. He say nothing. I say Are you afraid? He say, "What's going to happen?"

Now I'm asking you. What's going to happen?

Why are you sitting there silent?

Are you holding him here? For questioning? What kind of questions? How can a man kill with a smile on his face? How can you sit there in that chair and stare at me, and fold your hands in your lap, when there are two thousand men burning falling screaming, and an ocean on fire. Two miles from here. How can you sit in that chair? Is there anything useful you can do? Can you drive me down there?

Are you afraid? Of smoke or fire, of bombs, of dying, of war, of Japanese, of others, are we afraid of each other?

We should be down there, we should be with the fire and the smoke, we should be cutting the men out of the ship with our hands. We should all be down there helping. All of us. I'm not useless. Are you? I'm not afraid, I'm not made of stone. Are you?

Are those your car keys in your hand?

Can you take me down there?

The Deepest Part of the Creek

MARGARET BALDWIN

The first time I saw death
was with Alice Jane Newby.
She lived across the street.
She called me over to play that day.
I said I couldn't
'cause Alice Jane scared me.

She said *yes you can.*
Nu-uh. My mom won't let me.
Nyuh-huhhh.
I saw her just now in the A & P
she was headed to a tennis match.
I asked if you could come play today.
She said, That'd be just fine, Alice Jane,
so sweet of you to ask.

So I went.

We played
in the driveway.

I wanted to play Barbie dolls,
but Alice Jane wanted basketball.
Barbie dolls.
Basketball.
Barbie dolls.

Basketball.
Barbie dolls.
Basket—
  I said I don't wanna play basketball it's a stupid game!

So Alice Jane spanked me.

And I cried.
'til her maid came out
in her fake leather slippers
and told me to do
like Ms. Alice Jane said.

We played horse.
It's a stupid game.

You stand at different parts of the driveway and you free-throw,
and every time you make a basket you get a letter,
and the first one to spell the word *horse* wins.
I couldn't get past the "R."
Alice Jane got to "S."
You throw like a girl, she said.
I am a girl, I said.
No, you're not.
You're a HOR. H-O-R. HOR.
That's not how you spell it.
Nyuhhh-huhhhhh.
Her ball swished again.
She said *"E." I win.*
And I could see Alice Jane get an idea.

Come on—no wait—stay right there.
I did like she said.
Alice Jane went inside.
She was gone a long time.
It was *hot* in that driveway.

I wanted to go home
so bad it hurt me
but I didn't. I knew
she'd come find me.
She would. So I stood there
sweating and waiting
for Alice Jane
to come back out
and tell me what to do.

Finally she came out
with a pair of her mom's pantyhose.
They were dark. Darker than
the pantyhose of most
white ladies
because Mrs. Newby
liked to tan year round
in those suntan places.
(And Alice Jane swore
on her Bible
that her mom wore
nothing but skin
plus her goggles
when she lay
in her suntan bed.)

What're those for?
I said.
Close your eyes,
she said. And I did.

She tied those pantyhose
tight round my eyes
so tight you couldn't
wiggle your little finger inside.
It was like being blind,

but hotter.
Come on.
She grabbed my arm.
Wait. Where're we going?
You'll see, she said.
I can't see. I'm blind. Ow!
Take off your flip-flops, stupid.
The driveway's too hot.
Come on!
She started to run.
I can't run, I'm blind!
I'm blind. I am
but somehow I'm running
behind Alice Jane
holding on for dear life
off the pavement and onto the Newbys'
freshly mowed lawn,
over the pinestraw island
past her mom's roses,
now past the little pond
where we once
swallowed goldfish,
past the azaleas
thick with morning glories,
past honeysuckle smelling
like communion wine,
holding on for dear life
still running still blind
down into the woods
where we suck muscadines,
where my feet
find the path
where somehow
they know
how to go
without stumbling

down the hill
down the roots
down the dirt
down the wet
down the down
to the dark down
deepest part of the creek.

I got two things to show you,
says Alice Jane.
Can I take off the pantyhose?
Nope, you gotta come here first.
She leads me up
to an old log fallen
'cross the creek.
The log's thick with moss
and it smells like wet leaves.
Sit down, she says.
Now scoot on out to the middle.
But what if I—
You won't fall in.
Straddle it. You won't fall in.
I do like she says.
The moss scratches my thighs.

Now ride.
Ride?
Like a horse. Just ride.
So I ride.

I can hear my breathing
and I hear Alice Jane's.
I hear the mosquitoes
and the creek trickling under my feet.
And something
something

down there
starts to tingle.
You feel that?
I feel it. What is it?

That's your organism.
What's that?

Something that grows on you
when you're doing it and it
gets big and makes you holler.
I've seen it on late night.
Oh. I stop riding. What if I don't want one?
Then you can't never have sex.
Never?
Nope.
Oh.

That's the first thing, says Alice Jane.
What's the second thing?
Hold on.
She takes off my blindfold.
I blink.
The world's never looked so green.

Look down,
she says.
I look.
My spine shudders.
There's Alice Jane's white cat
Snowball lying on the black rocks
like he's taking a nap in the sun
only he's underwater.
What's wrong with it?
He's dead, she says.
I found him here this morning.

16

He hadn't come home in a couple of days.
I didn't tell nobody when I found him.
He looked so peaceful like.
Not a scratch on him.
It felt like it was a secret.
So why'd you tell me?
I don't know.
I say, Alice Jane, you scare me.
She says, *I know.*
And she starts to cry.

So now, when I think of death
I think of Alice Jane Newby
and how I made her cry
without even trying.
And I think of her mom
lying naked in her suntan bed
and her white cat dead asleep
in the deepest part of the creek,
how seeing it made my spine shiver
and how I ran blinded by pantyhose
down deep in the woods without stumbling
and rode some old mossy log like a horse
'til I felt my organism start to grow
between my legs
for the first time ever.

And sometimes?
It still tingles.

The Wet Nurse Sings

MARGARET BALDWIN

ACT ONE

THE PLAYWRIGHT: They want me to do a Chekhov piece.
Sure, I say, What sort of thing would you like?

Oh, you know, just something *Chekhov.*
You *do* know *Chekhov,* don't you?

Of course I know Chekhov. Everybody knows *Chekhov.*
I refer to Chekhov on a regular basis. Even to myself.
Even when no one is listening. I enter a room, I say,
Look, the woman on the chaise lounge.
She's so *Chekhov.*

This thrills and impresses them.
Yes! That's so Chekhov!

They don't even say what play they're doing.
They assume. They always assume you know.
And they speak in code . . . a shorthand of names
with too many syllables, elliptical references,
woeful sighs: We're struggling to find our *Anfisa.*
But you should see our *Kulygin Ishkavanovich Treblekev Potanov*—
he's really coming along. Oh, and did we have a
      breakthrough today
with *Masha* and *samovar!* We really *know* her now.

At that point you really can't say: Now . . . which play is this?
Because, if you do, their faces will shift imperceptibly.
And you'll know that they know that you don't know Chekhov.

ACT TWO

(The playwright's voice, recorded, speaks stage directions from The Three Sisters: *A clock strikes twelve. Masha quietly whistles a tune.)*

So now I'm reading *The Three Sisters.*

(Playwright's voice, recorded: She stops.)

Someone gave it to me in *Chekhov: The Major Plays.* It's a small book. He only wrote like four plays. Four measly plays.

(Playwright's voice, recorded, spoken quickly: Two men laugh. Masha resumes whistling. Someone plays the piano. Newspaper pages turn.)

Still . . . I'd never read it.

(Playwright's voice, recorded: An embarrassed silence)

Because . . .

(Playwright's voice, recorded: Crying, laughing through tears)

(Crying, laughing through tears) Because . . . Because . . . I'VE NEVER READ CHEKHOV!

(Silence. Playwright's voice, recorded: Murmur of astonishment and disapproval)

I haven't had time. Maybe I had time once when I *had* time unlike now when I really *don't* have time. But I never got around to it, okay? I mean, there's that *name* thing and all the flipping back and forth, and to be honest, I don't even like reading plays, not even my own plays. *I hate them.* So when I'm forced to read them like now, because I'm doing this *Chekhov* piece . . . I skim the dialogue and just . . . read the stage directions.

(Playwright's voice, recorded, wooing: Combing his beard, waltzing alone, hitting his plate with a fork)

I'm almost to the end of act two.

(She listens to the stage directions for the first time.

Playwright's voice, recorded: A bell rings. An accordion plays from the street. The wet nurse sings.)

Chekhov gives great stage directions.

ACT THREE

It's not like I haven't *seen* Chekhov. I saw *The Seagull* once in Montana! Sort of. It was an *adaptation*. They called it *The Meadowlark*—that's the state bird of Montana. I was living on the couch of this Buddhist forest ranger. He was the first Buddhist I'd ever met, or forest ranger for that matter, and we got stoned in front of his altar and went to *The Meadowlark*.

It was performed under a tent in the back yard of some *local actors*. People I'd never met. They were going for a western theme. The mother person—whatever her name is—she was a rodeo star. I can't remember the details, but she wore this leather ensemble complete with bright red boots and cowboy hat, and she did an unfortunate singing number with a rope.

November in Montana. It was wet and thirty-four degrees. The propane heaters were so loud they had to turn them off so you could hear that Nina girl . . . before she kills herself? And you *still* couldn't hear her because she *mumbled* . . . but you could see her breath . . . and her pink hair—she was going for this punk rock thing—and I remember feeling really, really sorry for everyone involved, except the mother, who I wanted to shoot.

The only reason I'd gone in the first place was because I was hoping, for some perverse reason, to run into my ex-boyfriend who'd dumped me for a girl he'd met on a *fishing boat*. I thought he'd see me and realize what a mistake he'd made. But he wasn't there and he never realized and I think they're married now with three kids in Kentucky!

And I was miserable. And the Buddhist was bitter. And he couldn't stand art or artists or plays, and had greasy hair and small pointy teeth, but I considered kissing him anyway.

ACT FOUR

(Stage directions are now sounds: A clock striking twelve)

(As clock strikes) So! Now I'm still carrying around *Chekhov: The Major Plays* trying to finish *The Three Sisters* so I can write this stupid Chekhov piece. And I'm late leaving work because

the receptionist just gave notice and the billing has errors and the copier's speaking in code. Now I'm rushing to the store so I can rush the groceries home before rushing to see a play that I don't even want to see.

(Sound of woman whistling "Rain, Rain, Go Away")

(Underneath whistling) Standing in the checkout line, in my gray swingy skirt and sweater set, I'm thinking: If I could just get back to Montana.

(Whistling stops) Where I had space and time to live on people's couches and brood about bad Chekhov and bad love and bad teeth. *(Pause)* But you can't go back. You can't leave your life. *(Whistling starts again. Grows)* I know this as I watch the checkout woman scan my soy milk and tamari roasted almonds.

I know this as she hands me my checkout tape that says:

If you're happy tell a friend!
If not, tell me.
My name is . . . *(Whistling stops again. Pause)*

Her name has way too many syllables. And her skin is dark caramel, and I don't know where she's from and I'm embarrassed I don't know and embarrassed *she's* checking *my* groceries and smiling—sincerely smiling—like a *sincerely happy person,* when all I want to say is I AM NOT HAPPY—*Anfisa Kulygin Ishkavanovich Treblekev Potanov*—I am SO NOT HAPPY. *(Pause)*

(Piano fade in: quiet, melancholy, Russian)

Instead, I swipe my cash card. She gives me cash back. Offers to help me to my car.

(Piano fade out. Collage sounds start: City sounds, street sounds: traffic, sirens, bus, etc. Voices laughing, shouting. These build to a cacophony underneath the following.)

Now the car. Rushing. Out of the parking lot onto the street past my office building, listen to *Marketplace,* fumble for CD, rush in and out of lanes to keep moving—anything to keep moving. Caught behind a bus.

(Silence)

Standstill. That's when I see her—the woman on the over-pass—one of those with a chain link fence that curves out over the highway? She's wearing a grey swingy skirt and sweater set, and she's standing . . . on the wrong side of the fence. A man in a grey suit talks to her from the sidewalk. People turn their heads as they walk by. She's got two fingers hooked into the links, and her body makes an arc as she swings down closer to the man.

And in that second before the bus moves, I think . . . the space between us is so . . . small. What takes her there? What keeps me here? What is she saying to the man in the grey suit? How long will he stay with her? How long would I stay? What will he say to his wife when he gets home? *(Pause)*

If only we knew. *(Pause)*

(City sounds soft, reprise)

The bus moves. My cell phone rings.

A man whistles in the car next to me. My cell rings. *(City sounds fade.)*

An accordion plays in the street. *(Slight pause)*

The wet nurse sings.

Excerpt from *Patty Red Pants*

TRISTA BALDWIN

PATTY RED PANTS, a twenty-six-year-old woman, is telling a story from her childhood; she is telling the story to the audience. She begins by speaking directly to them until she is transported back into her memory.

PATTY RED PANTS: I'm standing at that place behind my house, that place on the edge of the woods, and I'm lookin' down there. Into the woods. I've never been. The woods aren't too thick in this part and I can see—there's no one there. And I just—well, I see a trail—and—I follow it. I'm in the woods now, and Oh. My. God! I can't believe this is just outside my house! I can't believe a place like this can be all dangerous—it's so pretty. I'm following the trail and—it looks like a campsite—a circle of rocks and some burned stuff. Some, like, burned pictures of women—porno pictures. Matchbook, ripped label on a Budweiser bottle, this woman's pubic hair in the girlie magazine is, like, staring at me— some burnt old beer cans—Oh my God, I'm like, on sacred "guy ground."—I wonder what the—I don't know—the boys—looking at these naked girls, how the boys talk, how their hair and their clothes and their hands—I hear a sound. Twig snaps? My heart jumps. I hold my breath. And I—I have no idea why—my hands are goin' up my shirt, they're shakin' like crazy, and I'm—I have no idea why, but—I'm taking off my bra. It's a totally stupid bra, it's like an ultra-white, Cross Your Heart, came-in-a-box, totally embarrassing bra, and I'm standin' there holdin' it in my hand, I'm lookin' around, and—and I—I don't know—I hang my bra on this tree—and I *totally book.*

 . . . A couple of days later, I go back into the woods—I go back to that campsite—and I find my bra—in the dirt—with two holes burned into it—where my nipples would be.

23

Spinning

TRISTA BALDWIN

JESS, a single, decidedly urban woman in her thirties, sits alone at a table in a bar. Jess has had a number of drinks already, with friends who have left the table. At the start of the monologue she is speaking to herself.

JESS: Shit: Spinning. Not good not good. Those damn—what-doyacallits—taste too good. Get a grip, girl, shit. Right. Grippin'. A sticky ass table. End of the night table—is it last call?

(Catches a waiter)

Excuse me! Are you bringing drinks, I'm lookin to get another drink. What am I drinking, kamikazes, yeah bring one for me, and one for Japan. Because they're Japanese, baby, yeah!

(Waiter is gone.)

And change the music, what is this shit. Techno beat to some eighties song? You know you're getting old when all the music reminds you of junior fuckin' high. Old . . .

(Pulling a compact out of her purse)

Face. Shit face. Changin' shape. Mutable. Mutational. Nose slippin'. Eyes changin' direction.

(Changes direction)

Shit, what am I doin'? Everything/nothing. Shit! Shelby! That's it, what I need, Shelby, yes yes yes yes.

(Digs her cell phone out of her purse and dials)

Girl where are you when I need you—

(Gets her)

Shelby! Oh my God, girl, where are you? It's Jess! Jess. What do you mean where am I, I'm in town, girl! I'm down at (where am I?) Joe's Garage, or some shit. That's right, all the way from fuckin' New York City. Had to get out of there. Didn't you hear? Red alert! Closed all the bridges. Motherfuckin' Mrs. Bush came to town, and fuckin' what's his ass, Ridge. Tom motherfuckin' Ridge came to thank me for comin to fuckin' work. Citibank. Right. Fuckin' terror alert cocksucker what the fuck ever, time for a fuckin' vacation. So where the fuck are you and why aren't you here? Ha ha! Well come to— fuck yeah I'm drunk, too drunk to fuck! Shit, seriously, girl, I'm changing shape here, you gotta come here, you gotta see this, I don't know what I'm gonna do tonight, don't know what I'm gonna say, anything/everything, I almost kissed Katie, girl. You know it. Then Greg came over, and I don't know what I woulda done if—uh, I think maybe I should throw up. Should I throw up? Before I drink more. Like the Romans, baby, yeah! Shit. Wanna slip outta my skin tonight, girl. I know you know what I'm talkin' about. 'Cause I've been feelin' boxed up, boxed in, you know what I'm saying? This fuckin'—New York shit, it's, I mean there's M-16s on the fuckin' subway platform. Full on military—God, I can't think about it.

Come down here, would you?

Could you come, Shel? I'm just about to peel—rip this motherfuckin'—clothes, skin, naked down the street—what could happen? Buck ass naked blood screamin' down the street. What could they do to me? Maybe a night in jail, shit whatever. I mean it ain't like we're livin' in fuckin' Afghanistan, there ain't no Taliban motherfuckers, they wouldn't shoot me for that shit. God I gotta—

(Laughs)

Drunk girl streakin' down the—I mean it's not like we're livin' in Mexico, at least I'm not a fuckin' Catholic. Fuckin' Catholics and their Inquisition-havin'-child-molester-father-fuckers.

(Laughs, then collects herself)

I feel . . . "how I feel," you're my therapist now, Shelby! Fuckin' therapy. Amazing. Think about it: we're in a time and place where we can actually care about our feelings. Treat with importance, *Our Feelings.* If the bombs were falling on *us?* If all those Islamic fundamentalists descended like starved rats on us

25

flesh-baring, heavy-drinking females and our beardless sex partners? Our feelings wouldn't have much to do with life, then, would they. If the veils, the fear, the fuckin' madness took it all.

Maybe my face is—maybe I don't recognize myself because I can be so many things. Can't I? I'm free, right? I'm really fucking free. (Until I'm not.) I'm free until I'm not. Fuck, girl. Don't you think about it sometimes? We could suddenly *not* be *free*. Like all those people before us that were not free, we could could suddenly be—I mean what I'm doing right now could be a fuckin' crime . . . Sure, I know, sure, we're not really free and all that, this country's going—but it's not gone—and I—we—can speak our fuckin' minds, we can fuckin' do what we—Now think. Think about what time and place we coulda been born into. And we're here. Now. Shelby, what should we do? What should we do with all this? Something, right? We should really do *something*. Besides work at fuckin' Citibank (motherfuckers). And shop, fuckin' spend it so we gotta fuckin' go to work again and again, round and round. We gotta *do* somethin'. I just feel it slippin' away from us, and I'm livin' halfway, screenin' it out, burnin' time, but I got this energy. Don't you? Don't you feel it? Come on, Shel. Come out, girl. Come out tonight. Come with me.

C'mon. Let's get out there. Come out. And. And we'll fuck every motherfucker in the fuckin' bar! We'll fuck the fuckin' beer bottles, smash the fuckin' glasses, baby. Start a revolution, bitch. Mother-bitch revolution.

C'mon. You ready? Meet me. C'mon.

Excerpt from
Voices Underwater

ABI BASCH

JENNIE: The stream behind the house. I walk the gravel path, dirt collecting in the fringes of my skirts. Trees bend beneath heavy rains, the old oak tree, branches bending down. Look around. No one else but me. Lift my skirts ever so slight, they weigh me down with waters. Touch my toes to water, brown and deep and muddy. Slippery rocks beneath, shadows shift through water I watch fish swim by. Remove my skirts, one by one by one by one by one, blouse and all that's left beneath is. My undergarment.

Daddy would kill me if he found me like this.

I dream of that pair of eyes behind the oak, brown and deep and muddy like the creek, wish he'd watch me swim. Think on him, those eyes he hides, hair falling over them in golden folds, rain freckling his skin, his voice beckons me from behind the old oak, whispers me under his spell, his tongue like a lizard's. I am afraid and tickled all at once. That boy. That dirty dirty boy. Water against my skin and shiver inside my bones. Oh to feel the heat of his glare in the rains beneath the old oak.

Dirty dirty boy. Your eyes burn holes in my skin, you are a monster.

The screams at night are the worst. From my window I see fires in the distance past the old nigger cabins, sometimes hear things breaking out there. I try to shut my eyes so tight I get a headache, stick my fingers in my ears 'til I think I'll pop the drums and block it out.

It is raining outside. I wonder how they will set the fires. I hear them downstairs, growing loud and slapping on the back and laughing, then voices moving out to the drive. They are handsome. They are brave. They are a brotherhood of soldiers.

Sometimes I wish I was a soldier. When I see the fires in the distance I do.

My Daddy, he is their general. But when they leave the house I know there will be screaming.

The grind of the crank as Daddy starts the new Model T, loves his new Model T, first on our street, hear him tell Mama every day since he brought it home.

And the motor booms and starts and spatters and spits. And I know. The brotherhood is off to battle. White knights. They protect. Again there will be fires in the distance. There will be screams.

I toss and turn, try not to think on it.

Hours and then screams melt away. Try to sleep, my mind is elsewhere, on the back porch of the pawnshop and the boy I know who sits there who is a monster.

You must know these things.

Excerpt from
Lucy Dies in Fives

ABI BASCH

LUCY: Lights and voices lights and voices stifling hot. STAND BACK STAND BACK why won't they LISTEN.

So quiet why'd it get so quiet.

Hello?

I'm lying on a corner, on the pavement bleeding and waiting, waiting for them to come get me. They will take me to the hospital where they will sew me up and send me on my way. Or I will stay in a room full of bouquets—long lost relatives, friends from middle school will find their way to my hospital bed, and I will look to my bedside and I will see—Where's Simon?

If only these MORONS will clear away from me, give me space so hot so stifling hot, I'm shot, they can get to me and sew me up.

Hello?

Speak out loud Lucy speak. Hello. HELLO.

Can't feel my mouth. I feel my mouth I mean I feel it but. Hand, raise. Hand raise and touch mouth. HAND LIFT AND TOUCH LIFT AND TOUCH HAND TOUCH.

Lips tingle, touch them. Touch them, hand TOUCH.

(She gasp-screams, quick intake of breath.)

My lips feel my lips, touching my lips, other lips it feels like on my lips, on my face, I can't touch, but feel feel the lips. Simon? No not Simon stop. Where is Simon NOWHERE.

(Another gasp. She grabs her heart, a sharp movement.)

My heart you press my chest don't break my heart.

(She gasps.)

I can't. Fight back.

What if I'm dead. Oh God I'm dead, I'm dead.

I'm not dead. I'm thinking. My brain is moving. I had a—. A student. Had a, a student said brain activity, she said after the body dies brain activity continues for several minutes, five maybe, less, I don't remember, Mr. Kim taught her that in bio class, she said. Mr. Kim Mr. Kim Fuck you Mr. Kim.

Hello?

I have five minutes five minutes. Less now.

(She gasps.)

Stop crushing my chest you idiot it hurts it hurts my heart.

I have a brain, brain activity continues for minutes five maybe, hello? A voice just one would help me please. Hello. I am Lucy I am a school teacher I was shot I am bleeding stop the bleeding blood is red I remember red all color washed out now, eyes open, open eyes OPEN. I cannot see.

(She gasps.)

Lips touch, lucid and dead lucid and dead, Hello. Voices make it stop.

So quiet inside my head make it stop. Make a sound.

Mithridatism

PAUL D. BAWEK

LEE, a self-made businessperson, has made concessions in her life that leave her questioning her identity. In this pivotal scene, Lee finally confronts the man she loves with his racist world view.

LEE: You don—*(Lee breaks down. She collects herself.)* I know you think of me as white—but I'm not white—and honey you can keep on trying to convince yourself we're not different and love changes everything, but when we leave this room you'll still be white and I'll still be "other." That's the bottom line. And it's not just the world outside this room that's prejudiced, it's you Frank—because as long as you only see me and accept me in your white perspective you'll never truly see me. So don't tell me you're not prejudiced until you're willing to put yourself in my shoes and see the world from my point of view. Don't tell me you're not prejudiced until you come out from around the illusion that we're all the same, because we are not the same. This is a white man's world Frank and I am not white. And you seeing me as such negates my entire existence. If you see me as white, I'm not here. I'm nothing to you. Because I'm not white Frank! I'm "other!!" And I know you give money to charities to help the "other," and you love the "other," but you only do it so the "other"—including me—will rise above their circumstances to be more like you. White like you! And that, Frank, is the worst kind of racist, the one who doesn't even know he is.

Dot's Valedictory from *St. Luke's*

ANNE BERTRAM

Batavia Girls Academy, Batavia, Illinois, 1931, DOROTHY (DOT)
HENDRICKS

DOT: Batavia Girls Academy class of '31. I stand here, your vale-
dictorian; I stand here, looking out at your familiar faces. Some
of you I may never see again. How can I tell you what you have
been to me?

Some of you have come to me to share your joy at your
academic achievement, when your average soared with your
deserved high marks in chorus or home economics. You have
inspired me to apply myself all the harder to my own little
endeavors in algebra and German.

Some of you have invited me to glory along with you in
your triumphs of the heart, your fingers graced with handsome
rings and your plans a maze of gowns and flatware patterns. You
have fired my determination to find my own sphere of success.

And some of you have been kind enough to wonder what
the future might hold for me. For indeed, my studies have been
dry and my social achievements not conspicuous. I am happy to
tell you that I have been accepted for training at St. Luke's Hospital school for nurses in Chicago, one of the finest schools in
the nation. There, I will pledge myself to the same service as
that great lady, Florence Nightingale. It is a difficult service, a
humbling service, not well-regarded by the world. But, Nursing
is an art, as Miss Nightingale herself has said, it requires as
exclusive a devotion, as hard a preparation, as any painter's or
sculptor's work; for what is the having to do with dead canvas

or cold marble, compared with having to do with the living body—the temple of God's spirit?

And so, classmates, we go forth, each to the future she has chosen, each to the reward that she can earn.

Thank you.

Doll House

WILLIAM BORDEN

Do you know why I became an architect? When I was a little girl, my dad got me this two-story doll house, with a wall missing, and my grandparents gave me little furniture to go in it, little chairs, and a little refrigerator. Little people, too. One day I pretended the people were moving, and I took all the furniture out of the house, and I put it in my brother's toy Mayflower moving truck. I pushed the truck out the front door, across the sidewalk, over the curb, and into the street.

A car came along. The people were killed. I forgot to tell you, I put the people in the truck, too, so they were killed. I went back inside, and I looked at my empty house, and I felt really great. Like I'd accomplished something. I made up new people, imaginary people—a mom who was never tired and a dad who never got mad, and me, the little girl who was free to do whatever she wanted, and there was no dumb brother and there was no dumb dog.

I'd think, this room could be bigger. And wouldn't it be neat if there were two flights of stairs? I'd make all these changes in my imagination, until it was a completely different house. I drew pictures of my new house.

"What's this?" my dad asked one day. "Are you going to be an architect?" "What's an architect?" "An architect does what you're doing there." That's when I knew who I was!

In the eighth grade, the boys took shop and the girls took home ec. One day I snuck into the shop. I saw the T-squares hanging on the wall. I saw the triangles, the protractors. I went to my teacher. "I want to take shop," I said. "Girls don't take shop," she said, pleasantly enough. "But I'm an architect!" "You can be an interior decorator," she said, "you can decide where to put the furniture in houses." "I don't think there should be any furniture in houses!" I cried. "I don't think there should be people in houses!"

I killed the little people in my doll house.

They had it coming.

White Girl from the Projects from *Talking Masks*

CARLYLE BROWN

WHITE GIRL: Yeah, I'm a white girl and I live in the projects. You got a fucking problem with that? If you say you don't, then you're full a shit, 'cause everybody's got a problem with that. Niggers be calling me "Sparkle." What do you think they would call me? Latifa? And to white people, I got to be some kind a ho. Well, all a y'all can kiss my black ass. That's right, my black ass. 'Cause you see, I identify. Except where I'm looking in the mirror, or looking at my mama, all I see is black. My best friend is black, my boyfriend is black, my neighborhood is black, and the people I hate, and the people I love, the ones I can trust and depend on, they ain't nothing but black. So what am I suppose to be, a white girl? I don't think so. And yet everybody wants to give me a hard time about who I'm suppose to be. And niggers? Niggers, they're the worst. Calling me Sparkle and shit. I tell my boyfriend,

"Who hails the damn cab when you can't hail one? Who tells the police, 'No officer he ain't bothering me, he's with me.' Do I let your ass walk home or get locked up? No, I play the white girl and save your fucking ass."

And bitches, bitches be all up in my shit.

"Ooo look at Sparkle. Yeah girl, Sparkle can dance, she got rhythm, she's blacking down girl."

Soon as I say something, bitch be up my face, talking 'bout,

"Say what? I'll fuck you up white girl."

I tell 'em,

"You better get the fuck up out a my face, 'fore I make your ass wish you was back in slavery."

That usually chills everybody out, 'cause a real white girl would never say that shit. You see I grew up in the projects. The project's all I've ever known. Came here with my mama when I was little. Now, my mama she don't like her no niggers not even a little bit. She says God is showing her how low she's fallen to put her here among a bunch a poor, low niggers. She's sitting up there in that little, tiny ass apartment all by herself, don't speak to neighbors, ain't got a friend, surrounded by nothing but niggers, and she wants to tell me how I'm all fucked up. Of course nobody messes with her. They better not, she may be white, but she's my family, she's my mother and I don't play that shit. Besides, who would want to bother with some old miserable, negative ass white woman who hates you anyway? Life is rough enough baby. When I was a little girl first come to this neighborhood, and all them little black bitches come to vamping on me just 'cause I was white. Who come standing up in the middle a all a them but Lucille, and Lucille say,

"Get your nasty asses away from her. She's a friend a mine. She's with me and if you bother her again I'll have every last one a your nasty asses."

I understood right away, standing there scared with tears in my eyes, that no white person had ever done a thing like that for Lucille. And from then on I knew what it was to have a friend. And from then on I tried to be one. Yeah, that Lucille she used to be schooling me jack, with that raspy ass Bessie Smith voice of hers.

"You got to fight back Sparkle. You got to throw down. People always gonna come down on you if you different and they think you weak. So, you got to terrorize 'em, you got to pulverize 'em, you got to kick their fucking asses, you got to let 'em know that, that weak ass little white girl they think they fucking with ain't you."

Yeah, Lucille, that's my girl . . . The worst part though was the brothers. White girl suppose to be the easy piece a ass. Ain't that a bitch, after all they been doing to sisters for hundreds a years. Quite naturally the sisters want to say I deserve it, 'cause I'm suppose to be the revenge liquidator for the entire white race. I mean, what I look like? Just for the way I look that mean I don't want a hold hands and be in public with somebody I like, instead a having them sneaking around to see me, or stepping off the sidewalk when we together and they see their friends, acting like I'm not even there. Lucille told me her mama, who got a raspy ass voice more like Bessie Smith than even Lucille, she say,

"You don't need no little dick man, whether it's between his legs or between his ears."

As soon as Lucille said it, I did it.

"Forget them niggers."

And don't you know as soon as I decided to have nothing to do with them brothers, they did everything possible to have something to do with me. Jay Man, Roger, Sonny Boy, Ro-Ro. All them boys coming after me, I was in heaven girl. Only thing was all of them Rudy Poot motherfuckers wasn't just looking for a girl, they looking for a white girl. Niggers was talking to me all of a sudden like they was trying to sound like James Bond and shit. And where as they would tell a sister to go get it for herself, they telling me,

"I'll get it for you baby."

I don't know why, but I didn't like that shit.

"I mean excuse me? You may be looking for a white girl, but I'm headed in the other direction my brother."

No, the cats I liked they wouldn't have nothing to do with me. The cats I liked, them brothers were really black. Why was they black? They was black because they were proud of who they were. They wasn't thinking about being with no white girl so they could be accepted by anybody beside those who already loved and respected them. And those people were black. And if they was gonna love me, I had to be more than somebody you could see when you're looking at 'em. I had to be somebody you could see inside. And for a young white girl in my neighbor-

38

hood, let me tell you my babies, it could've been a very foolish thing to do. Now, when this body was young, this body was fine, finer than it is even now. But, I couldn't pump that up. I'd just get the easy white girl thing all over again. No, I had to be down. So I read. I read James Baldwin, Alex Haley, Malcolm X, Maya Angelou, Claude Brown, Sonia Sanchez knocked me out. I even read Eldridge Cleaver's *Soul on Ice*. What a piece a shit that was. Talking 'bout, rape you a white girl make you a revolutionary, get yourself a codpiece, go home to your black queen so she can wait on your lazy ass hand and foot. What an asshole. But, Michael J. Johnson, who lived in my projects, now there was a black man. Michael J. wasn't black just 'cause he was born that way. No, Michael Jay was black, as he would say,

"By a process of conscious self perpetuation."

Who he was, what he was, how he was, was the product of the struggles, sacrifices, and achievements of his people. Man, I loved me some shiny, blue-black, nappy headed, Michael J. Johnson. You hear me? Trouble was Lucille liked Michael, too. And the problem was that Lucille wasn't into none a that.

"Why we got to talk about being black all the time? I know I'm black. I don't need nobody to tell me I'm black. Yeah, the world sucks. Things are the way they are and there ain't nothing we can do about it. So, why we got to talk about it all the time?"

Lucille wasn't into none a that, what she called "black stuff," yet still Michael Jay was on her like, you'll excuse the expression, "white on rice." And what Lucille liked Michael for I just don't know. I mean, yeah he was fine, but ain't who you are the same as what you believe in, how you behave in this world, how you live your life? I was totally getting into what Ralph Ellison was talking about, only I wasn't the invisible black man, I was the invisible white girl. Ain't that a bitch? What the fuck you going to do? Life's got to go on. Right? So, I marry Ro-Ro and we have us a baby girl. That was cool, until Ro-Ro found himself somebody who really wanted to be a white girl. Now he's done gone, happy as a rat in a cheese factory. My baby girl, little Lucille, she half-white, she so confused.

Who wouldn't be? In the end things between Michael and big Lucille just didn't work out. Hello. Surprise. You are who you are. But I miss talking to Michael, being around him. He made me feel in my skin like I was dark and luscious like a soul sister. Now Michael done gone to parts unknown and Lucille stills blames me to this very day.

"Always jaw boning with my man about some movement. I got your damn movement. I'd like to get some movement myself. I'd like for you to get some movement in some other direction and away from my man. That's the movement I'd like to see. Why don't you go out and find yourself a white boy."

White boy? You believe that shit? A white boy, what I want with some white boy? Do I look like I got some 'only white boys need apply' sign on me? Just 'cause I'm very, very light skin that means I got to be condemned to living with white folks for the rest of my life? No, no, no, I'm not down with that. You see I believe that all them brothers sitting up in jail doing big time for nickels and dimes is an injustice. All these young bloods out here sick and dying from being shot up with bullets and drugs, I think it's a crime. Aid to the Third World and AIDS in the projects. They be shooting 'em up in the suburbs and they be talking 'bout, how did it happen here? And just by saying so, we know that they know that it's always been happening here in the projects. You think I want be somewhere where people are complacent about shit like that, and not outraged. No baby, not me. 'Cause maybe when you look at me what you think you see is a white girl, but deep down inside me, I'm Black.

Excerpt from *Little Vines*

CORY BUSSE

A house. ANNIE, *thirty-five, looks pensively over her shoulder. She closes a door behind her and tries to light a cigarette. She can't get the childproof lighter to catch. She shakes it, tries again. Still no good.*

She cocks her arm back like she's going to throw the lighter across the room. She stops and composes herself. One more try, and it lights.

ANNIE: Two weeks ago already. Two weeks ago, I lost the man I loved most in the world. All clichés apply. One minute he was here, the next . . . car accident. Another car crossed the median. It wasn't his fault from what I can gather. But a car accident. It just seems so common. I mean, here was this guy. Funny. Beautiful. Smart. God, he was smart. He used words like "abstruse." Not just "abstract." Not just "complicated." Both at once. He was precise. But—and here's what made him amazing—he could pull it off. He could do it without sounding pretentious; that's not an easy thing to do. And he gave everybody he met credit for getting it, too. If they didn't, he had this soft, teacherly way of using the word again in context. Not dumbing it down, but really making sure he was understood. That's what made me fall in love with him in the first place.

(She takes a long, illicit drag on her cigarette. She stares at it for a second, then crushes it out on the sole of her shoe.)

I was sitting in a bookstore coffee shop in one of those huge, awful chains that every pseudo-intellectual in America swears they will never go into. We vow that we'll support the little, independent bookstore on the corner, the one that lets a cat roam around loose. We rail against the corporate machine that's invading even our quiet spaces and swear that we'll never be sucked in. We boycott and proselytize and take a stand. That is, until we realize that the big chain stores take Visa and serve turtle mochas. So, I was sitting drinking a turtle mocha that I'd paid for with Visa when he sat down in one of the squooshy arm chairs across from mine. We both played at not noticing one another for a little while. I'd peek at him from behind my magazine and look around like I was scanning for a friend I'd come with. I'd bust him gawking as he flicked his eyes away the second I glanced in his direction. He may have been beautiful and perfect, but he was still a guy, after all. Then, just like that, he started talking to me. He asked me if I'd read *High Fidelity.* Not seen the movie, which would have been an easy question to ask. He asked me if I'd read the book. It was this great thing. It was this vote of confidence. He gave me credit for having read the book. Which I hadn't, but that's beside the point.

(Pause)

When I first found out he was dead, I felt like I was going to throw up. I called his office. I was just calling to say good morning and to tell him that I was home and that I loved him. Charlie, my son, was sick and I was home. Somebody, a woman, a voice I didn't recognize, just picked up his line and told me, "I'm sorry. He was killed in a car accident this morning." I honestly don't remember much in the moments immediately after that. But I've thought since then that she shouldn't have done that. The news must have been brand new to his assistant, or whoever, for her to just pick up the phone and tell me he was dead. I must have called during that exact, silent moment after they'd gotten word and before they had done anything. That's how I found out—on the phone with his secretary—that he was killed in a stupid, common, car accident.

(Pause)

I remember the first time we made love. Ugh. He'd roll his eyes at me when I called it that. He hated that term. I don't know a guy who doesn't, actually. This is one of those times when his vocabulary was the exception, not the rule. He wasn't vulgar about it, though. He didn't insist on calling it "fucking" or "screwing" or whatever. Not unless it was, you know, right. In the moment. Appropriate. I guess he'd refer to it as the first time we "had sex." So I remember the first time we had sex. I was feeling guilty as hell. I'm Catholic, of course I was feeling guilty. The guilt is the only thing we kept from Judaism. I felt bad, but I didn't want to stop. I kept pulling him on top of me, and then making him stop. The poor guy didn't know if he was coming or . . . not coming.

(She laughs hard at her own joke.)

It ended up being not—for both of us—that first time. I called him the next day, and I told him, "I only feel guilty if I have time to think about what I'm doing. The trick is to keep me busy after." He burst out laughing—this great belly laugh like I'd genuinely meant to be funny. He said, "So you're okay if we have sex, just so long as afterwards we get you a part-time job and a hobby?" And he just laughed. It wasn't a big deal.

(Pause)

The day I found out, I had to run and lock myself in the bathroom so that Charlie wouldn't hear me cry. I thought about what I was going to say to him when, inevitably, I broke down in front of him. I knew I would. It's the same reaction I had when I used to be hurting and I would see my mother. All she had to do was say, "Oh, honey," to me, and I would dissolve into uncontrollable sobs. My children elicit that same reaction in me now. But now, two weeks later, he's in the ground. He's gone. And I didn't even get to say goodbye. He was perfect and I loved him. I keep making myself say "was." He "was" perfect. I keep messing up and saying "is." I keep saying "love" instead of I "loved" him. And even that sounds cheap and wrong because I do love him, and I'm so pissed off that something like death makes me have to use the past tense. I want to say that I love him. I want to tell everyone that I love him and that he is perfect. I want to tell Charlie why I'm so sad. If nothing else, I want to tell someone, anyone, what's making me cry all the time. But I can't. And I'll never be able to. I couldn't even go to the funeral. No one I know even knows who he is. I can't even mourn. I have to keep it all inside, and it's killing me. I've never once spoken his name aloud, not even to him. We agreed, it was too dangerous. We used only pet names. Safe names that would transfer easily from each other to our spouses, raise no suspicion. Honey. Baby. Sweetheart. If I mentioned him to a friend, it would be like he were imaginary. Like he never existed. Which, of course, he never should have. Not in my life, anyway. But he was perfect. And I loved him.

Excerpt from *Tumor*

SHEILA CALLAGHAN

SARAH, late twenties, is two months pregnant.

SARAH: Walking around the women's department in Macy's. There are children everywhere, crawling like arachnids, they have more legs than I thought children were supposed to have but I guess you start to notice these things when you've been hijacked. Looking over their sweaty heads for something simple and angora I recall when angora was simple, when the angora gaze was not flecked with knots of unfiltered mess who run for no reason and stick to everything and wail like original sin multiplied by twelve.

I keep my eyes a safe distance above the swarming ick and spot a garment worthy of my once-upon self. I move towards it as smooth as a rollerball pen. Soon I am close enough to attract its static cling. My hand, electric, rises to the rising sweater arm, also electric, and in our dual reaching pose we are an Italian Renaissance masterpiece. But as my fingers splay for the grasp I feel an icy sludge make its way down my left leg.

I hear this: "It's not my fault, the bottom fell out!" And then a small person is galloping away from me towards a larger person. I look. My entire calf from knee to ankle is covered in a seeping red liquid. Pooling into the side of my sneaker is roughly eight ounces of bright red smashed ice. And lying next to my foot is a Slurpie cup with its bottom in shreds.

That night I dream of buckets and buckets of blood gushing from between my legs.

Excerpt from *Kate Crackernuts*

SHEILA CALLAGHAN

A female role originally written for PAUL'*s voice. Paul is a young, sickly looking man. He is pale and transparent.*

PAUL: Okay. The story goes like this. Her name was Mother and she was mine. She spent most of her days shrouded in a shrivel of herself which grew tighter and tighter by the day, and I watched it happen. She was sick, you see, sick on a stick in that stylish chronic way people like to talk about from their throats instead of their mouths. I held her hand when she couldn't walk, then held her cane when she couldn't stand, then pushed her around when she grew wheels. Father was also shriveled, from sorrow not sickness, and couldn't help. Brother was a coin flipping itself, no help either. It was me and me. But Mother was so radiant and weightless, wrapped in her affliction like cotton candy, and her pretty sickness was forever aglow.

And one day I looked at her and the candy had melted and she was a sticky lump of Mother in a bed and the sheets were damp and clung to her like they were searching for something beneath her flesh and she cried out Paul I'm sick and I said I know and she said no it's different this time and I knew but pretended I didn't.

She kept a black felt tip pen by her bedside for me to keep track of her medicines and at this moment she started shouting out words, words that made no sense, random snatches of sentences she could not form or colors she could not pronounce and I reached for the pen on the dresser and couldn't find any paper so I began writing her words on the skin of my arms and when I ran out of arms I took my shirt off and wrote them on my chest and when I ran out of chest I dropped my trousers and wrote them on my legs and then she ran out of words and her lips turned blue.

So I leapt into the bed and held her, she was moist from the struggle of trying to make sense and I was moist with tears, and I stuck to her and to myself and when they pried me from her we were both covered in swirls of black ink and not one word she uttered survived our separation.

I haven't been able to feel my skin since then, Kate. Do you know that feeling?

Gertie's First Day in the Nursing Home

JOAN CALOF

GERTIE is in her room talking to a staff nurse.

GERTIE: You like my outfit? You know what the director of the Home tells me when I go play the piano for the old folks here? "It's not appropriate garb. Leggings are for teenagers." A *chaleria* on her. This top and bottom are pure cotton, from Chico's. I have three outfits, coral, turquoise, and purple, my favorite color. Let her tell the inmates of the Home what to wear. She'll never tell Gertie Cohen!

I'm so lonely since my Abe died. And I've lost so many! My friend Rose. Smart. We used to meet for tea, but when she got blind she couldn't go anywhere. And that lovely Englishwoman, what was her name? When her husband died she walked around whistling. These women with unhappy marriages, they're sometimes better off when their husbands go. Me, I loved my Abe so much, I didn't think I could stand it when he went. Such a loving patient gentle man. The good go first.

No one even touches you. Maybe they think old age is catching. To tell you the truth, this growing old is for the birds. I don't like to cook, the meals on wheels are *feh*. A woman comes to give me a bath and wash my hair once a week and someone comes to clean, but she doesn't even move the furniture. I wear this big black ugly thing on my wrist so if I should fall. About all I can do is dress myself. Here I can play the piano without having to take a taxi, company all the time. See, I don't put my children through the wringer. I decide myself.

Besides, they live so far away. I started to volunteer when my Abe went into the hospital. I played at that hospital and he would sit in the back and listen. He was proud of me. After he went, I thought I'd go crazy, so I volunteered all over town playing the piano. Jazz. I played the piano since I'm nine. In the twenties I played on the radio, and in the forties I played boogie woogie. When I was eighty, eighty-five even, nothing kept me from my gigs. I took buses in thirty below. But now I take a taxi. You know, once they offered me to play in a piano bar, but I told them no. Why? The piano faced the wall.

You want to hear me play? It's like a country club here. Tablecloths and people to eat with, people to talk to. And I know about the floors, too. First and second are for those who have all their marbles, third for those who still have some marbles, and fourth, don't ask. The higher the floor, the fewer the marbles. And the solarium is beautiful with plants and a waterfall. You should have seen the gardens I planted. Laid out the whole plan, knew the heights of all the shrubs, and all the flower beds trimmed in candytuft. Anyway the only trouble is with that waterfall you can't hear a thing anyone says. My friend Eva is on second. She loves it here. Plays cards three times a day. Me, I don't play cards, just piano. You know, Eva was one friend who talked sense. Not a stupid woman like most of them, all they can talk about is their aches and pains and their grandchildren. Eva is still smart, reads the paper, listens to the news. Me, I watch *JEOPARDY!*, Ted Koppel, do crossword puzzles. Good for the brain. I have another friend here, Sally, but she's lost her marbles, she's on fourth. We once shared a little cottage in Miami, she was always turning off the lights. A cheapskate, stupid, but a good-natured woman.

One thing I don't like: the recreation director. I ask her to play the auditorium and she says Becky Gittelson has been playing there forty years. What do I care about forty years? Gittelson bangs, makes clinkers. So I tell her, I'm an excellent pianist and I'm good enough to play anywhere. I write out lists of all the places I played. Here, I'll read it to you: fashion shows at the synagogue, nursing homes, the hospital where my daughter was born and my Abe died, I played there fifteen years, got a pin for

49

volunteering, I played mother-daughter teas, American Legion, Lion's Manor, Hebrew Sick Association, even the psychopathic ward at the Veterans' Hospital. What an audience! You should hear them sing "Don't Fence Me In." That recreation director says I can play once a month. Once a month! Gittelson plays every week. And I know all the oldies: I want my name in the elevator, just like Gittelson. That Gittelson, they should chop off her hands! . . . I'm no fool. I don't say that to anyone.

If I don't get to play, I'll die.

Excerpt from *Journey to the Center of the Soul*

JOHN CARTER

A play about the relationship of Freud and Jung. This monologue is delivered by SABINA SPIELREIN, *twenty-one, a former patient of Jung and now a medical student and his protégé. She is presenting her thesis to Jung, who has recently terminated an affair with her.*

SPIELREIN: I write not about death. I write about yearning to die. Here, listen.

(She goes to a spinet and plays a transcription of the act two love duet from Tristan und Isolde.*)*

It can all be heard in the music. Tristan yearns to die. He and Isolde, they are drunk on love. Chord by chord their love constructs their death. Nothing else matters. Not even honor. Death they welcome. Where else but in death is love eternal? How else but through love can death be survived? You see, they cling to each other, love and death, she and he. When you make love to me, I experience in every cell the wedding. Then you go home, and it seeps out. We are not drunk enough, my Tristan. We are not willing even to be dishonored. I long for your hands on me, now as I play. I could tempt you. I could turn you to my will, but my will fails me. Frau Emma's love is better. She loves you for what she gives you. I love you for what you give me. I would devour you, and what then?

(She builds to the conclusion of the music.)

But only the ghost of you in my bed now. How sad my nights.

Excerpt from *First Lady*

ERICA CHRIST

EVA PERÓN: What is a woman in Argentina? A mother. A good woman is a mother. A good woman does not get involved in politics.

If she does, she's a whore. If she's lower class, she's a whore. If she's not married, she's a whore. If she doesn't have children, it's God's punishment for being a whore.

(Pause)

Those oligarchs really like that word.

(Pause)

There is a rich ladies club, the *Sociedad de Beneficencia*. And traditionally they invite the First Lady to be the honorary president of this oligarch club. But, of course, since I am such a terrible example of First Ladiness, being, in their minds, a whore, they refuse to ask me to be their honorary president. The note says, here, that I am so young, their society is more suited to older women. My note to them says, here, that they would perhaps be more comfortable inviting my mother, in that case, to be their honorary leader. I will send it today. Tomorrow I will secure the deed to their building. Then next week I think I will evict them and dissolve their organization and confiscate their funds.

(Beat)

I deposited money in a Swiss bank account under the name Eva Maria Duarte de Perón, while I was First Lady. My husband fled in exile two years after my death. His usurpers attempted to get my money out of that account, filing documents that said I was the deceased wife of a former president of Argentina and therefore my money was state funds. Remember what I said about that name, Duarte. Well, since Eva Maria Duarte de Perón never legally existed, she therefore could not have been the wife of a former president, and therefore could not have a bank account with state funds in it. There are those people who wished that I had never existed and the only one who shares this fantasy with them is my Swiss bank account!

(Beat)

I don't know how to add for inflation . . . but it was equivalent to . . . roughly seven hundred million dollars. When I died in 1952.

(Beat)

It's still there.

(Beat)

I may need it again.

(Beat)

At least I'm not a stupid whore.

(Beat)

Oh we had such a good time. At one point, I had to close down the newspaper, *La Prensa.* Then these ladies suddenly became concerned with freedom of speech, and protested outside the offices of the newspaper, demanding that it be reopened.

(Laughs)

I had them all arrested and thrown in jail for a couple of days, the same jail which housed the prostitutes. They talked about whores so much, I thought they might like to see what a real live whore was like.

(Beat)

And people said I had no sense of humor.

(Beat)

But what, I ask you, could possibly be funny about the sufferings of millions of people! If I am to attend to that, I really don't have time for joking around, for parties and dinners! I go to the opera, once in a while, but that's it! Juan and I have a lot to do!

Excerpt from *Break*

BETH CLEARY

LOU, a widow in her sixties, has been a custodial worker for twenty years. She is nearing retirement but on her lunch break today she tells her friend Mel why she is ready to walk out today.

LOU: So on 6 A.M. break, I was standing outside the back door having a cigarette, and Sammy comes out. He's got a cuppa coffee, we're talking. Six A.M., pretty windy, barely light out, just nice, beginning to come up, you could see it through the trees. So we're talking and watching, and there's birds, and he tells me his son made the football team in high school, and I say great, and he asks me about my grandkids and I tell him good, most of 'em got jobs, you know, all that.

And then Sealey drives up to around back, down the end of the lot near the Dumpster, he don't see us I'm pretty sure, there's that overhang. And I see him taking a big stack of papers out of his front seat and looking around to make sure no one's around and he sees the coast is clear and he gets out and chucks the stack into the Dumpster. Which is pretty full. And me and Sammy duck inside the back hallway as he drives slowly by. When we figure he's gone, we go out, we don't even say nothing to each other, we go out and walk over toward the Dumpster. Some stuff's blowing out, and we're figuring some of it's the stuff that Sealey threw in. We want to see, what's our steward up to at that hour, he's on day shift. So we go over and pick up some of the papers that blew out. And we bring 'em back in where there's enough light. And they're those questionnaires we filled out last week about what kind of shifts we want, and what more benefits, and what can the union do for us, yaddyaddy. And Sammy's even got a grievance complaint in his stack of stuff. All originals.

So Sammy goes up to Sealey at his desk, after he comes in later with coffee and a box of doughnuts. And he says, Frank, uh, I found these in the parking lot, on the ground. They gotta be yours. Here. And Sealey looks at them, and he turns beet red and he says to Sammy, what are you doing, spying on union business? And Sammy says hey, I was walking outside on my break, and Sealey says he's filing a disciplinary on Sammy and to get out. He's elected, he's doing his job, Sammy's lucky to be in a union.

And then I, me, I get called in by Flynn, at 7:20, and he asks when I went on break. And I says I dunno, about six this morning. He asks if I punched in and out and I says yeah, you can check, and no one's ever asked me that in twenty years of working at Cutter. And Flynn says well today we're asking. And I says I want my union steward present if there are going to be any more questions. And Flynn says your union steward is out at a meeting, and I know perfectly well he isn't, 'cuz I seen Sammy in with him when I walked by, which I don't say. And Flynn says you better watch it, you've only got a couple years left, you don't want to ruin it with slack behavior at the end. He's seen that happen.

(Beat)

And I says . . . I says to Flynn, who'd I talk to Mr. Flynn, if I was interested in taking home one of these plants the company's going to throw out? Who'd I talk to, Mr. Flynn? And he says, what? And I says, since I'm in here, since you called me in here, after twenty years on the job and counting, and asked me for the first time ever about my time card which has always been regular and you know it, since I'm in here Mr. Flynn, I'd like to be able to take home one of the plants we're throwing out, I see them lined up on the loading dock, and I could drive around and take one, but I figure I'll ask since you might be proprietary as they say about the company's greenery. And he's taken aback, but he says I can talk to Physical Plant Services but he doubts very much if I can have a plant since they're company property and such. And I says well I've always wanted to take one of them perfectly good plants that's property being thrown out but by the time it's the end of my shift I'm not thinking about them plants I'm thinking about getting home and washing my uniform for the next day and putting my feet up, but since you called me in here today Mr. Flynn, for the first time to question whether I'm doing my job right punching in, staying within break time, what not, it occurs to me to inquire as they say, to inquire about whether after all these years the company might give me something they're going to throw away anyway, something I want, that wouldn't be trash to me. Something I'm asking for, on the day you're inquiring as to my loyalty. A plant that's trash to you, but'd be nice in my picture window.

(Beat)

He watches me real close and picks up the phone and calls Physical Plant Property or some office, and asks on the phone while keeping his eye on me about the company policy on discarded plants, whether they're free for the taking. And after awhile he hangs up the phone and says, "Sorry, Lou, it's Company policy, no removal of property by unauthorized personnel. You're not authorized." I stare at him. He goes on, "It's like the soap or the toilet paper rolls, we inventory all of that, you know, you can't take any even if it's discards." And I say Mr. Flynn think about this a minute, think about this situation real hard, first time I'm in this office in all these years, 'fact I've been here longer than you have, never was in Mr. Boyle's office here before you either, I've kept my head down and done my job all along, I'm just asking for a plant. It's not inventory any more, it's trash. Think about this, Mr. Flynn, think about this in a human way. And he says if it was up to him he'd give me the plant. No question.

And I asked if that was human enough, being human himself but enforcing a nonhuman policy. And he says I'd better leave his office, he'd called me off the job long enough.

Excerpt from *Hungry Ghosts*

BILL CORBETT

The wife, EMILY, *of a traveling pair of food critics, responds to her husband's condescending assessment of her.*

EMILY: We still work under the following assumption: that I am the drudge. I handle the mundane. I sweat the small stuff. I'm the maid, the secretary, the boot black, the cranky longshoreman. I am certainly the chauffeur. I do the driving; I do the heavy lifting, I scrub up the messes, I do the collating; I raise the children, I put things in alphabetical order, then go out and wash the car, because, after all, these are all *easy* things to do. Things you could train a gibbon to do. I manage the mundane, and—it would seem by your frequent complaints—not very well, at that. I am on thin ice, damn it, and I'd better watch myself. I'm the helper animal that you'd like to return to the lab. You, on the other hand—you!—my God, you, you're our *genius!* You're the irreplaceable part of our team. Myself? *Highly* replaceable—perhaps, as I mentioned, by a primate. You? The *source*, the light, the star by which we navigate. It's implied that a big bright genius at work sign floats over your head at all times. Your vast mind is constantly active, buzzing and whirring, collecting valuable observations and stunning imagery, putting together words in unheard-of combinations: witty, poetic, even transcendent, laboring to give humanity the gift of your unique insight. And though your mind—no, not just your mind, but your very *soul!*—though your *soul* is constantly at work for the greater good of us all, we less-evolved entities don't recognize this, ingrates that we are. No, even as you do the Great Work, we blinkered, literal-minded Neanderthals—well, our eyes see you as merely watching soap operas, or eating your third lunch of a given afternoon, or sitting in your boxers staring blankly out the window, or playing solitaire on your laptop, or tossing your depression medicine down the garbage disposal, or throwing up in the sink from one too many Cuba Libres, or . . . or! . . . taking the Ukrainian cleaning lady from behind, tossing a casual hello back to me as I come in the door unexpectedly, not missing a beat, your pants around your ankles, when in all those instances—and this is what we, the Great Unwashed, don't see, damn us anyway!—when in all those instances, you're actually *working*: producing the Magnum Opus, the work that no one else can do, no one in the world and really, very few can even understand. Our eyes are clouded because of our severe perceptual limitations: we don't recognize the act of a Creator, a god on earth, to whom the mortal rules don't apply, when we see it. What our eyes see is a lazy, neurotic shit with a sense of entitlement which would have shamed the Emperor Nero. But we know nothing!

Practical Jokes

JEANNINE COULOMBE

ANNA, forties, is about to sign papers to admit her mother, who is suffering from Alzheimer's disease, into a full-time care center. Anna talks to the center's admissions attendant.

ANNA: These are the papers then? To put her away. I know I'm not supposed to think of it that way, but that's how it feels. I'm sorry. This isn't easy for me. I'm sure you hear that a lot. At least I think you would. Or, should. Of course, yes. Sorry. Okay. Date. What is it? April first. Yes. Of course. April Fools'. Crazy April Fools'. Crazy. You know when I was a kid we actually celebrated, in a way. I mean, not like my mom would bake an April Fools' cake or make some kind of April Fools' meal or anything like that. No, just old-fashioned practical jokes. Mom always liked them. She was good at them. Clever. One year she came running up the stairs at 6 A.M., while all of us were asleep, I mean, it was only 6 A.M. My brothers and sisters and I were asleep. I'm the youngest of five, you know? Yeah. Two older brothers, two older sisters. I broke the tie. None of them live around here. Nope. Joke's on me. Oh, but that year the joke was on all of us. Mom ran up the stairs yelling, "Kids, kids, wake up, it's 8:15, you're going to be late for school." She always said she never saw five kids jump out of bed so fast in all her life. We dashed down the stairs and there she sat on the landing. Laughing. April Fools'. All my mother had to do was laugh and all seemed right with the world. She laughed and we all laughed with her. We got her back, though, the next year. At 6 A.M. we ran into her room yelling, "Mom, Mom, wake up, wake up the toilet's overflowing." Our toilet was always overflowing. Old house. Bad plumbing. Mom hated it. I think that was the worst thing about my dad not being there. Not so much that she was alone, but that she had to deal with bad plumbing. Of course, we were just kidding. She ran into the bathroom grumbling in her old blue nighty, carrying the toilet mop, still half asleep. We were all laughing. April Fools'. April Fools'. I know. I know I have to sign the papers. She laughed with us, you know. That year. She wasn't mad. She laughed. She always laughed, even if the joke was on her. Seems every day is some kind of April Fools' now though. I could tell her anything. It wouldn't matter. Could be 6 A.M. or 4 P.M., 8:15 or 9. April first or January fifteenth. It doesn't matter. At first I could deal with it. I could. She'd just forget dates or misplace her purse, little things. I'd just have to remind her a lot. Then, it was like I was always five to her and my dad was still alive. That didn't even seem so bad. But now it's like there isn't much of anything left and she wanders a lot. I've lost my humor about it. I'm worn out. It's nothing but cruel now. The whole thing. She raised us alone, so strong, so capable. And always laughing. Always. She doesn't laugh anymore. *(Pause)* Where's a pen?

Excerpt from *Life on Pluto*

STEPHEN R. CULP

MAVIS: I miss you, Pluto. You were always happy to see me. Poor little dog. You weren't the same after you ran head first into that nativity scene. You were running through the snow, barking at the falling flakes, not watching where you was goin'. You made such a crash. The baby Jesus was shattered into a million pieces. All the shepherds, the three kings, Joseph, Mary, and the heavenly hosts looking with wonder at an empty manger. Christmas wasn't the same that year. One night after too much eggnog, I went outside in my nighty to make a tiny little snowman. A snow Jesus. To give the plaster shepherds something to look at. When I was done, with Frosty the Snow Jesus all tucked in his straw, from out in the sky the biggest light in the universe shone down on the stable. Turned out to be the search light of a police helicopter, scanning the neighborhood for a Salvation Army Santa gone amok. But for a second there, sitting in all that light, I saw why they were looking at the manger. Somewheres deep inside those plaster heads, they knew Jesus was a melting lump of snow. And it didn't matter one bit. It was the looking that mattered. It was the looking. The plaster Jesus gave Pluto a concussion. He kept wandering off and getting lost after that, so we tied his chain to a tree. He'd run round and round. Round and round the tree, the chain wrapping around his circle getting smaller. Then he'd run the other way. The circle would get bigger, then smaller again. And now . . . now I'm all wrapped up in my chain. If my circle gets any smaller, I'll disappear. I'll just curl up and die. They'd bury me by Pluto. He was always happy to see me.

Excerpt from *The 13 Hallucinations of Julio Rivera*

STEPHEN R. CULP

DOROTHY: Excuse me, but have you seen a little black terrier? Are they gone now? Did you see where they went? Did they have a dog with them when they took off? I just know they got him. Toto's all I had left. We were trying to find Glinda. Saw her bubble fly this way, but she lost us round a tree. Toto and me sat down to rest for a minute when down they swoop! Smelly, disgusting apes! *(She kicks off her ruby slippers.)* Stupid shoes don't work. Don't even fit. Blisters all over my feet. And no one can be trusted here. Not even Glinda. Lies through her teeth. Click your heels, she says. So I do, right? Turns out she spiked my sarsaparilla with opium. Had this dream that I'm in Kansas in my very own bed, and everyone was there. Then I wake up in the enchanted forest. I've got a headache, and a couple of munchkins are playing under my dress. Filthy midgets. The Wizard was no help. He's a dirty old drunk. Made me play horsie on his knee, and his breath makes me want to vomit. Kept sticking his hand up my dress. Everyone in Oz wants to go up my dress. I hate it here. Even the Tin Man. Always asking me to oil him in a naughty place. So I let him rust and sold him for scrap. Oh . . . I'd stay away from the Emerald City if I were you. That place went downhill since they put the lion in charge. He hired the winged monkeys, who were happy to get jobs. I sorta melted their boss. Well, the lion gets his courage back, and remembers he's a carnivore. Has the winged monkeys fly all over, bringing back all sorts of munchkins and animals to eat.

Now he's got Toto. I thought they had me for a second there. Lifted me off the ground by my pigtails. But I grabbed their pee-pees and squeezed real hard. They screamed and dropped me then they crashed into a tree. Now they're hopping mad. But I won't let them take me. I haven't made it this far to be chopped up and fed to that awful lion. *(Pause)* It's a very long road, mister. Very, very long. Anyway, Kansas is the dream. Not Oz. I'm stuck. And to top it off, the winged monkeys take my little doggie. Poor Toto! Mind if I ask you a question? You don't look Ozian. Where are you from?

Excerpt from *Anna Bella Eema*

LISA D'AMOUR

IRENE speaks.

IRENE: My name is Irene and I have been alive here in this trailer home for as long as I can remember. When you are alive in one space for such a long time the things that you remember mix with the things that are happening now, and the things that you dream about. What I mean is, sometimes the things that are happening are equal to the things that are not happening. So as I speak to you please do not ask me to come clear on such points as "happened," "did not happen," "is happening," "will happen." They are all simmering in one pot. Here on the electric radar range inside this trailer home.

You can see I am a thick woman. Look at my wrist. One time someone tried to poke a stick through this wrist, in order to pin it to the ground. They poked and poked and poked but the stick would not go through. The scar is long gone, as you can see. This kind of thickness goes for the rest of my body too. Look at my ankle. Look at my waist.

Here is the timeline of my life: Birth. Learn to talk. Learn to read a little. Learn to love. Learn to walk (yes, very late). Father is leaving. Learn to watch my mother smash bottles. I am gaining weight. Go to school. Math. Learn how to not get made fun of. Camping out with the kids in the trailer park. Learn how not to love too much. Pull the thick braids of the rich girls. He is smiling at me. Darkness and breathing in dust. Mother, I feel a bird fluttering. I am having a baby. Look at her beautiful teeth! I am fifteen and then now I am twenty-five.

(She considers the audience.)

Here we are.

Excerpt from *Anna Bella Eema*

LISA D'AMOUR

ANNABELLA, a ten-year-old girl, speaks about her home.

ANNABELLA: We have been living in this trailer park for as long as I can remember. I suppose I was born here. A lot has changed since then. As you can see, we are the only trailer left in this trailer park. I guess that blows the park part. But there used to be more.

(The actress playing her mother takes out a small tape recorder and presses play: sounds of a child's trailer park play-world.)

Victor lived one home over with his mom Val. Victor was one year younger than me and a fucking horny bastard. Nine years old and all he ever begged for was blow jobs. I told him I'd give him one if he'd kiss me with his mouth open like they did on soap operas. He thought that was way too gross so we were both out of luck. Across the dirt from us was Chris and Curtis Crystal and their mom Charlene. Charlene had inherited a luxury trailer from her grandmother and one whole room was filled up by this big white circle-bed. A bed in the shape of a circle! When Charlene would leave on her boyfriend's motorcycle, Chris, Curtis, and I would spend hours and hours playing space station or ferry boat or Las Vegas Show Girls on Parade. I have never seen a Las Vegas show girl but Curtis has and he showed us how to put on the fishnet stockings he stole from Dollar General and the feathers he gutted from his pillow. There was also Joanie and Forrest and their mom Brenda-who-cried-all-the-time. And Misha, Alexis, and their mom, Masha, who came to our trailer park all the way from Russia. Everyone was outside all the time. Or piling into our home for story time with mom. Or daring each other to kick the plywood nailed to our trailer home to see what would come running out. It was a fun life. And then they were gone.

(Silence. The tape is turned off.)

Something is coming. It's either the interstate or the end of the world.

Excerpt from *16 Spells to Charm the Beast*

LISA D'AMOUR

LILLIAN, a sophisticated metropolitan housewife, speaks to her tabby cat as she waits for her very late husband.

LILLIAN: Between you and me, tabby, I'm glad we've had these four days alone together. Swapping spells, admiring the view. Don't tell Ned.

(Lillian face reads: Well, that shouldn't be a problem. She half sings:)

Towards the beginning of time, when the ocean dried up for the first time, at the bottom of the ocean, they found the bedraggled tabby cat. Is it dead they cried is it dead? No it is not dead they said. Its soul is living temporarily inside the body of a wise and sophisticated metropolitan housewife who indeed might be the Woman Who Sees All Things so do not desecrate the body of this tabby cat do not encase its five appendages in glass no leave the tabby cat there on the dried ocean bed until the tabby spirit returns to the tabby body and relates to us the Wisdom of the Woman Who Sees All Things place pillows of finest silk under its head and vases of exotic herbs around its four paws and tail no do not touch the tabby cat do not touch it if you feel you must touch it come on the designated day and you will be given the proper gloves and the proper hat and you will be allowed one touch in the proper place in addition we will build an emerald replica of the tabby cat that is slightly smaller than the real tabby cat and the devoted will be allowed to come and kiss the replica that's right kiss the replica—no don't be disgusted this is a very holy ritual consider yourself lucky—and so the people did all this and in addition small clusters of the devoted were sent on pilgrimages to seek out the Wise and Sophisticated Woman inside whose body the tabby cat was living, the Sophisticated Woman Who Sees All Things. Now these small clusters of devoted pilgrims had very few funds and very few possessions and so in order to survive they formed the Cult of the Tabby Cat, attracting curious customers with their curious wares: they sold small pieces of jewelry wrought into the shape of the tabby cat they sold restorative ink enhanced with the oils extracted from the hairs of the tabby cat they sold handkerchiefs which held the impression of the tabby cat's tail and in this way they made their way and in this way they also formed their long-term plan for finding the Wise and Sophisticated Woman Who Sees All Things for they knew that their wares would one day from the natural and somewhat random progression of market trends become fashionable and therefore expensive so expensive that only Sophisticated Metropolitan Housewives could afford them in this way would they narrow down the field of possibilities in this way would they find the Wise and Sophisticated Woman Who Sees All Things the Unassuming Eye that holds the soul and secret of the tabby cat and so the pilgrims voyaged and sold their wares and the faithful at home tended to the body and surrounding altar of the tabby cat and made effigies of the tabby cat out of dirt, snow, and sand, and chanted the chants of the tabby cat and developed mystical numeric systems and ecstatic purrs based on numbers and purrs found in the tabby cat and one day—

(Ned enters. The spell is broken. Lillian stands. Ned glowers.)

Excerpt from *16 Spells to Charm the Beast*

LISA D'AMOUR

NORMA, Lillian's daughter, is hugely pregnant. She speaks to her mother, Lillian.

NORMA: Mother, don't say a word, I've decided there are things you must know.

I want you to meet your twenty grandchildren.

(Norma introduces each child. Each child is represented by some inanimate object, objects which, for the most part, are small and hand-held.)

This is number one, Reginold Rust, his father's only son and the sickliest of the bunch. See how he coughs as though he is hacking up the weight of the world? See the track marks on his arm from numerous, painful, long-term IVs? So many times has Reginold begged us to let his life slip away but his father wouldn't hear of it, no his father insisted that he be kept alive and even whipped poor Reginold for whimpering about his fate.

These are Regina and Gina Rust, the first set of twins and the most giddy. So giddy they were kicked out of preschool for giggling it up during a lecture about mummification. I mean you would think they could keep their little mouths shut and when I asked them about it all they could say was Mummy please someone has to find the humor inherent in the ritual I mean really liquefying the brain by injecting a serum through a straw inserted in the nostril? One day we will be canonized for our giddiness and they laugh and laugh they are difficult to tell apart but I think Gina has inherited your shallow breathing.

This is Regenerate Rust who assumed the shape of a brown cardboard box at an early age, becoming a living aberration of the phenomenon of natural selection.

This is Reggie, Reggie, and Reggie Rust, triplets whose names are distinguished by the increasing force with which you roll the "R" which initiates their name. This, and the fact that they are girls with names traditionally given boys guarantees them a life of misery and humiliation . . .

(Noticing Lillian's attire)

Were you getting ready to go out? No? Great, I'll continue.

Next is Regingerbread Palm Rust (nickname Doom Palm Rust), a boring girl, actually, subverting the duplicitous possibilities inherent in her name, she sits around waiting for the sun to hit just right so she can trim her toenails in comfort.

Reginrummy Rust stinks of peaches and fancies herself a poet.

These are Ginny, Ginseng, Regensburg, and Regent Rust, who have taken their quadrupleness seriously and make every one of their mistakes four times each, which forces me to deal with their mistakes a total of sixteen times each and each and every time I need to deal with that look on their faces, that blank, befuddled look that says Mom we don't know how this happened, we are completely baffled, it must be something inherent in our genetic makeup, it must be some fierce genetic mishap passed on to us from you, who received it from your mother, so really we have no Will of our own, and even if we exerted that nonexistent Will we would have to do so four times each and then think of how much more miserable you would be.

Gingival Rust was born with lime green gums and spends her nights tormenting her sister Doom Palm by making up characters named Doom Palm who are far more lascivious and interesting than the actual Doom Palm.

Gingersnap Rust oh fuck it she's so transparent you can figure her out for yourself.

GIN, Nig, and Gin Rust are a triptych of sisters which, when they stand in the proper formation, tell the story of one of our forgotten family matriarchs, a matriarch who YOU NEVER TOLD ME ABOUT, MOTHER, a Madame Veronica Vanderlay Davis, who discovered neon in her makeshift chemistry lab which she assembled in the basement of her bungalow only to be swindled out of her discovery by a certain Samuel Lemkins, who convinced her that neon was not a rare, inert gaseous element but was actually quite common and already in everyday use in Tajikistan and parts of the Orient. And when she realized that she had been swindled, when she realized that Samuel Lemkins was taking credit for her discovery did she weep or sigh or pluck out all her hairs? Did she exile herself to the top of a high rise apartment building? No indeed she did not she swallowed her pride and took to the streets, as a roving instructor of young girls, and let her beard grow long and her wisdom grow thick and she is still to this day honored in certain countries as a Woman of Great Regard, unlike you, mother, and unlike me, your daughter and if you had told me earlier about Madame Veronica Vanderlay Davis perhaps I would have made a few different choices in my life, choices which would not have resulted in my bearing twenty children within ten years, but, no, really I don't mean that because I am so so so grateful and thankful for GIN, Nig, and Gin Rust who, through their birth from my womb, have introduced me to this family treasure and everything I might have been.

(Pause. Norma is really exhausted and freaked out, but neither Norma or Lillian can say anything. Norma continues.)

And these are the two Lillians Rust.

One has crystal blue eyes and the other emerald green.

Lillian the first likes to read Louisa May Alcott and Lillian the second prefers Dickens.

They are each enrolled in piano lessons, and charmed the audience to the point of real tears at the last piano recital with their rendition of "The Entertainer."

Lillian the first likes gymnastics.

Lillian the second likes bikes.

Which makes them a real human interest story, seeing as Lillian the first is missing her right foot and Lillian the second is missing her left.

And that's the whole lot.

Excerpt from *Kuwait*

VINCENT DELANEY

A military press briefing during the Gulf War, 1991. MARTHA, *a Pentagon spokeswoman, appears at a lectern. She addresses us.*

MARTHA: Good morning! I see some sleepy faces out there. You all get coffee? Could be your last chance. Let's get started. You all bring your checklist? Page one, please. You've got five gallons water, insect repellent, sunscreen, UV protection factor forty. Some pale skin out there. Compass, GPS system, locate your position down to six meters. We're sixty-three miles and twelve feet from Club Med. Which unfortunately is a smoking crater. This is like summer camp, isn't it? Who brought a guitar? Now most important, you'll want to wear this. Government ID, identifies you as a certified noncombatant. I suggest you have it round your neck at all times. If you take fire, you'll need to show it. Hold it up high and point to it. Show me. Get your hands up. Do it. Do it now! Good. If I were killing you I would now stop. Kevlar vest, takes anything up to eight millimeter rounds. Above that you'll need to duck. That's a joke, feel free to smile. Stay close to your escorts, and you won't fly home in a box. Or boxes. You have freedom to observe, interview, photograph, and report everything you see out here. Once we read it first. Anybody have a problem with that?
(She smiles, picks up a pointer.)
    I have a treat for you folks first. Who remembers *Top Gun*? Oh, I'm no Tom Cruise. I know it's true, you can stop. We've prepared a little surprise. This is actual video from the nose of the bomb itself. We use a disposable camera. That's a joke, feel free to laugh. We are now able to deliver munitions with surgical precision. I've always hated that metaphor. Surgery is blood and gore, when you think about it. Surgery is not surgical. Our

smart munitions, on the other hand, are what surgery wishes it could be. Roll footage.

(She gestures at an invisible monitor.)

This is what the world looks like if you're a bomb. Simpler. This is—was—an enemy command post, which for devious reasons was placed next to an orphanage. You will have trouble telling them apart. Watch now. We're zooming in. And down. Anybody got nausea? Grab onto something, we're coming in fast. Completely ignoring the orphanage, zeroing in on the window of the—now look. Look! There's a guy coming out of the target, see that? He's standing there thinking—come on, don't think too long, buddy. Get out of there! Get out! Move! Good decision. Luckiest man alive. Because now here we go! This is it, baby! Yes! Yes! Yes!

(Beat; awed)

Look at that. Look at that. Precise, efficient, no collateral damage. That is what we call one smart bomb. If I had children—which I don't—if I had any, and they were orphaned, God forbid, if they had no maternal parent, and lived in that orphanage, you know what? I would feel perfectly safe if the US Army bombed the building next door. Those babies are safe, thanks to our bombs. Not one of them but rolled over in his sleep. Nighty night, little Arabs.

(Big smile)

Any questions?

Work from
Nosegays on Monday

MATT DI CINTIO

MARGARET, a homeless woman, middle-aged, speaks to Aaron, a chiropractor, outside a corner grocery in Midtown, New York.

MARGARET: I was the only person in my high school who chose not to go to college. Yeah there were lots of people who chose to do other things besides college but I chose not to go to college. I wanted to work. I wanted to get up on Monday mornin' 'n go to work 'n come home 'n be too tired to do nothin' 'n go to bed so I ken get up in the mornin' 'n go work again. I wanted to do anything. I started out a receptionist for a veterinarian, but I got tired of seein' things go in alive 'n come out not at all. So I switched to a doctor's office. Least there livin' things come back out. Usually. Whatchu do? You git up in the mornin' 'n go to work 'n come home 'n be too tired to do anything 'n go to bed 'n git up 'n do it all again. That's right ain't it? Ain't that usually the case?—I ain't got 'ny degrees 'n we all do the same thing. Up, work, down. Up, work, down. Only difference is, I did it sooner so I'm gon' do it better 'cuz I'm gon' do it for longer. 'N that's a good thing 'cuz I wanted to work.—I'm talkin' like I got a job. It's stupid to think about, nothin' makes no damn sense. I wanna work. I don't care what it is. I just wanna work. I washed floors, windows, dishes, cars, houses, served breakfast, served lunch, served dinner, waited on people, waited for people, drove people around, called people, wrote to people 'n told people how much money they got 'n what they ken and can't get at. I got experience. I'll do anything. I ken do anything. I just wanna work, I wanna work! I'll sew, I'll carve, I'll cook, I'll sell, I'll buy, I'll trade 'n I'll mop. I just wanna work, I wanna work!

It don't make no damn sense. Why won't they let me work? I wanna work. I don't want their money, I wanna work. Why won't he get his patent leather shoe off my back 'n lemme work. I wanna work. The brother in humble circumstances oughtta take pride in his high position. But the one who is rich should take pride in his low position, becuz' he will pass away like a wild flower. For the sun rises wit' scorchin' heat 'n withers the plant; its blossom falls 'n its beauty is destroyed. In the same way, the rich man will fade away even while he goes 'bout his business. But when 'm I gon' go 'bout my bizness? I wanna work! I wanna work! I wanna work I wanna work I wanna work I wanna work I wanna work . . . !

Look from
Training My Hands for War

MATT DI CINTIO

SUNNY, a young and unsuccessful prostitute with dreams of dancing, catches herself in her lover's mirror.

SUNNY: What are you looking at? Don't look at me with that face, I've seen that expression before, I've seen it a million times before. Don't think I don't know what it means. I know exactly what it means. All my life I've been trying to get that look on my face, and I just can't manage it. Maybe it means I have too much heart. Maybe it means I don't have any. My first lover, my only real lover, the one with dark eyes, painted that look on his face when he left me. It was that exact look, only his eyebrows were raised a little more than that. As if it were a surprise to him that he was saying goodbye. It was a surprise to me. It's still a surprise to me. It's that exact look my father wore when I told him what I needed to be: on my own, free, unbound, all those things, yes. But I needed to dance. I have to spend the rest of my life moving. It was the motion, it was in the motion that I was me. I have a vision in my mind of myself and whenever I picture myself I'm running. I'm running home, I'm running away from home, I'm running to the edge of the stage for my bow and my applause. And the look I have on my face is nothing anybody has ever seen anywhere before. Ever. It's the look of someone who's gotten to where they're going. Do you know that look? I sat across from my father with my feet in perfect fourth position—under the table my feet were on the floor but in my mind they were in the air in an arch I could have taught classes about. The only arch at that table was the one his eyebrows formed in confusion. He was, as the word goes to describe it perfectly, *bemused*. The poor

man who wore looks easier than he wears cheap shoes. The poor
man who tried so desperately to understand anything all his life,
through wide eyes and a quarter smile. Do you know that look?
No smile big enough to cause dimples, nothing big enough to
leave that kind of mark. But the eyes are open big and the forehead's made to suffer with a few crinkles. Yes, that look. The one
that looks like you're trying and you know you're trying. That's
the look you're giving me now.

Excerpt from *The Soft White*

PAUL DIOS

A withered, yet luscious meadow at the edge of a two-lane interstate road; a porch and the front setting of a rundown shack make for scenery in the background; tree stumps and logs are sparse and make for good sitting.

MISS AMERICA: *That night everything changed. There was enough dust on that interstate to make us feel lost, because at some point and I can't remember when, I felt his hands on my shoulder as they slowly made their way down my neck. By this point the bus is going in zigzags, I reckon. Don't know which way I'm driving while he kisses my neck and whispers in my ear, "Christ is in my underwear." So I start yelling, "We're gonna die, we're gonna die," but none of it matters. Instead, the bus goes sliding off the road, as I'm grabbed onto tightly from flying out. I tell him that I want out, but he can't listen, because the music grows louder, as I'm tossed out of the chair. I begged to get off and promised that I would never tell anyone about what had happened. Instead, I dropped my panties and hiked my skirt up like he had wanted me to. So I run to the back of the bus to the emergency exit and try to budge the door open. Just as I'm about to turn the handle, he comes from behind and slams me down onto the floor. I dragged myself up the aisle, until I caught flight and started running, but he's holding on tightly around my ankles like a deadweight.*

(Pause; frightened)

Oh, but then, he started to plow into me, spreading me apart like he were a shovel digging for gold. After he took his hands out, the smell of blood lingered on his fingertips while staining the ridge of my dress. By now, he is ramming his Jesus penis in me so that I can feel his manhood sting. He started off slow, making soft moans and groans, biting my chest like I were

79

some piece of meat while blood started to form a puddle around me. In my mind I thought, this is what it must feel like to finally become a woman.

(Pause)

When all was said and done, he walked back to the dashboard and started to smoke. Eventually, he would lower the radio and ask me to get up, but I tell him I can't. Instead, he lifts me up and steers me dead straight into the woods. We walked for quite awhile until finally we got to a pond and he's all teary eyed while stroking my hair. The last thing I remember was a fist twice across my face and boots slamming against the lower half of my rib cage. I tasted dirt for the first time that day. When the sheriff found me three days later, he gave a report on the news, saying my body was bruised in almost every crevice of my frame. The autopsy reported major injuries of hypothermia and a fracture from behind the head to the right side of my jaw. That caused some swelling and bleeding in the brain. I choked on my own blood. There were teeth marks on the back of my neck and all over my chest.

(Pause)

I once smelled pretty, you know.

Excerpt from *Viper*

STEPHANIE FLEISCHMANN

HELEN: When I die, I want to be burned in the fires of a crematorium. But I don't want my ashes kept standing useless in an urn. And I don't want to be scattered by the winds over the four far corners of the earth, either. Just to end up as dust on somebody's windowsill? No, uh uh. I want to be cooked up so hot my ashes turn; they crystallize. When I die, I wanna be a diamond. But not just a ring-finger diamond. To be banged about in dirty water when Janie does the dishes? No—I want to be worn around her neck. On a chain so tiny it's just about invisible. So I shimmer and shine every time she says a word. So she remembers me every time she breathes. Like I used to be. But I don't just want to be a *diamond*. I want to be a pencil, too. Diamonds, graphite, they both come from carbon. Graphite is an excellent conductor of electricity. It's expensive, I know, but I've got just enough saved, I think, to make it happen. So. There you go. A diamond it is. A diamond for Janie and there should be just enough of me left over for a pencil after the diamond's done. A pencil for writing Jimmy to write his words down with: So many words he'll write with the graphite pencil that is me, they'll add up to a book. He'll write and write until there is no more left of me but the book and a pencil stub he can put away in one of his little aluminum fly-fishing boxes. Stick it in a drawer and keep it for his kids when he has them—if he has them—so that his kids, my grandkids, lord knows if I'm gonna live to see them, rate he's going, so that my grandkids can sharpen the stub, and draw stick figures and cartoons in the margins of their books. With me.

Ask me—being made into a pencil is better than going to heaven.

It's immortality.

Excerpt from *Viper*

STEPHANIE FLEISCHMANN

BOBBY JEAN: On my way up here, back in Baltimore, I saw a procession of horses. White horses. Seemed like a hundred, but there were only six. Six white horses pulling a white carriage. Like Cinderella. Then came the limousines. White like the horses. Limousines and more limousines, and then the SUVs, white like the limousines, so many, it was like they were never going to stop. A river of white cars, whiter than clouds, stretching from here to kingdom come.

I stood and watched. And then I asked. Who's in that carriage looking like a fairytale? I asked. That's Jam Master Jay, said the man standing next to me. But he ain't no fairytale. Dead is what he is. Musta known he was gonna die. Because that's what he wanted, that's what he asked for: six white horses and a carriage fit for a prince. Everything in white. Right down to the Adidas. Shit.

Nobody ever ask me what I want when I die. And I ain't never told nobody, neither. So I asked him: What do you want? And he answered: When I die? When I die I don't want no horses. I want tigers. A pack of tigers, harnessed to one of them black hearses—coal black (don't see what white has to do with it)—put in neutral, hearse rolling along with the engine turned off. So everything is pin-drop quiet. So you can hear the sniffles. That's what I want. One of them black hearses with flames airbrushed on the chassy. Like I'm riding straight to hell. That's what I want when I die.

The Conversion of Inversion

DIANE GLANCY

An overwhelmed WOMAN *to herself in disordered thoughts. Setting: a rodeo arena.*

WOMAN: It has infested me. In sorrow I would bring forth children. *(Genesis 3:16)*

For a moment the house is quiet. What are they doing?

I been pushing the ground so long I can't get up.
I want to say run don't get married don't have children in sorrow but flee the country. Your desire will be toward your husband. You'll have barbed wire for a wedding band. You'll try to make it through the day until your cowboy comes home. He walks in the door. You run to him. He is tired. He is beat. He wants his space. He feeds his horse. He wants supper. He wants sleep.

The children wake wild in the night with dreams.

It was the underground water level that left the field marshy after rain.
He dug the postholes they filled with water.
He hit the ground with his shovel. Borrowed a tractor turned it over in the ditch.
The whole place floats.

But the old cemetery nearby—surely the coffins would rise.

Why he has to be off every weekend at the rodeo.
I am left with the children.

Not one of them ever quiet at once.

You see the road go down the hill like an aisle in a theater.
You can see a long way back to the farm where you spent your
childhood like a nickel, and it your last.

The clouds were flowered wallpaper over you. After that the
land flattened into April.

Somewhere the ceiling fan struggles on the screened porch. The
wisteria plays at the theater. A nickelodeon of wind all day.

Now the prairie is a dance floor that doesn't interest you.
Your Billy two-stepping on a horse.

All afternoon wind jangles the trees that lean to the north.
Under the cardboard moon.

You know the clash of heat and cold, man and wife, mother and
children.
It's your rodeo ride.

You walk late into the theater after the show has started. You
learn to feel your way down the aisle.

How did you get lassoed into this show?
How did you come into this theater in the dark, the aisle falling
like a prairie road over the hill? All the way to the front the
screen so far up you have to crick your neck.

You held hands in the picture show. You fell so easy.
You stumbled all the way to the front of the church.

It is not hard to be a Christian.
You have nothing here. You are married to an absent cowboy. You
have three small children. You feel yourself saddled. Cinched up.

You feel them on your back with spurs.
You buck at the rodeo all day.

The wind is your witness.
You know you need a savior who hung on a tree.
You would have believed it anyway.
You could feel the evil inside you. You could run and leave them without a horse.
You need a savior who could hang on the cross and come out alive.

Yes, get a woman juiced up, give her three small children night and day. The older brother hitting the younger when she turns her back. What if he grows up bigger than you? He'll beat you 'til his anger is spent. Don't you ever do nothing but hit and fight?

That I needed a savior was not news.
That I needed an outside source—

I felt my loneliness and betrayal.
I didn't know I would get an empty envelope for a husband. Wasn't it supposed to be different than this?

Above the porch swing, the whole world is turned upside down. The boards cross the ceiling like rows of crops in a field. The old ceiling fan rattles with thunder.

Excerpt from *The Plant Society*

CAROLYN GOELZER

The performer playing C *also personifies Moll Flanders.*

C *(Indicating an artificial geranium)*: This one is a fake. I purchased it from Jo-Ann Fabrics. The price tag on it said $29.99, but when I asked the woman to check to see if it was on sale, she came back and said it was $2.99, so I bought it. It came in a 15" ledge basket with "assorted greenery." *(Pulls out the plastic bag with the remains of the basket and greenery, and shows it to the audience)* When I brought it to the register, the cashier said, "It sure is beautiful," which really freaked me because I thought it was hideous.

When I got it back to my studio, I yanked out all the "greenery" and pulled out the hunk of "geranium" at the center. I trimmed it to look about the same size as the ones I've been growing. Then I potted it up in a clay pot with potting soil, with rocks in the bottom of the pot for drainage. I felt a little foolish doing that.

I think it looks remarkably real and like the others. The flowers are a darker shade of red than those on the ones I've grown from seed, and the petals are doubles, not singles, but I think on a good day this plant can pass. I labeled the pot, and measured the plant, and catalogued it in this journal where I record the data for all my plants. Here it is:

(Reading from journal) G32: 14"H x 12"W. 33 leaves.

It's been remarkably consistent.

This is Moll:
I've worn many disguises.

(C serves cups of hot green tea to individual audience members during the following:)

I posed as a Countess once. I outfitted myself with a rich Coach, 4 Horses, two Liveried Footmen, and a Page with a Feather in his Hat. All the Servants called my husband "my Lord," and I was "Her Honor, the Countess." We traveled to Oxford, and a very pleasant journey we had.

I drest me up in Widow's Weeds to escape Creditors, and call'd myself Mrs. Flanders.

I disguised myself as a Servant Maid in a Round Cap and Straw Hat, so I could inquire about a man I'd been living with, who'd grown very Sick, and had moved back in with his Wife.

I drest me up in Mens Cloths. I lived for a time as a man. I called myself Gabriel Spencer, and was a Thief of some Reknown.

I dress'd me up as a Beggar Woman, in the coarsest, most despicable Rags I could get. It was the most uneasie Disguise I ever put on. It was a Dress that everybody was shy and afraid of. Everybody was afraid I should come near them, lest I should take something from them, or lest they should get something from me . . . get a disease or something from me . . .

I sometimes took the liberty to play the same Game twice, which is not according to Practice. I never succeeded amiss, but generally I took up new Figures and contrivances wherever I went.

You know who you were when you woke up this morning. Since then, how much of yourself have you shared, or shown? Do any of us ever truly make ourselves Known?

(C and the audience members sip tea together for several moments in silence.)

Excerpt from *The Plant Society*

CAROLYN GOELZER

c: This plant is prayed for:
(C points out a healthy coleus featured in a small shrine.)
I wanted to say Catholic prayers for this plant because about half way through the book, Moll Flanders becomes a Catholic for a couple of weeks. I called one of my friends, who's an ex-Catholic, to advise me about what I needed to get started. She happened to be camping in the north woods when she got my message, and left me one saying I was fucking with her Serenity and she'd call me when she got back to the Cities.

So I was on my own. I decided to go to St. Patrick's Guild in St. Paul. It's a store. What a trip! It sells everything from ecclesiastical robes to BVM bird baths. It sells rosaries with miniature soccer balls for beads. There are rolls of Testamints in a box by the register.

I was looking for a short prayer I could say over my coleus, and a picture of the Madonna and Child that I could hang over it. I found the picture I needed in the half price bin. I really like it. The Virgin wears a crown, which is fetching, and the baby Jesus looks like a little girl. There is a canopy of gold stars in a halo over their heads.

The woman who rang me up at the register told me she couldn't believe that this particular Blessed Mary and Child was on sale. "$3.77!" she said, "Hallmark gets more than that from us for it!" I really didn't know what to say. I mean, what *is* an appropriate response?

She rang me up and then asked me if I wanted the Virgin in a separate bag. I was a little uncertain as to why she was asking me that—especially since the bag she'd put the picture in was plenty big enough for the other things I was purchasing. I began to wonder, a little paranoiacally, as a respectful nonbeliever, if perhaps the Holy Mother was not supposed to mingle with certain elements, being a Virgin, you know, and a religious icon, etc. At the same time I couldn't possibly imagine what I'd picked up at St. Patrick's Guild that could possibly give her offense.

For some reason my credit card was taking a long time to be processed, and the cashier and I had to wait for approval together by the silent machine for what seemed like an eternity. Finally, it went click click click click click and the cashier looked to me for a response about the packaging. I told her, "No, one bag is fine," but I scoured her face for signs of impropriety. She didn't make eye contact with me as she bagged up the items and handed them over. Her eyes were waiting for my signature on the bottom of the credit card slip, so she could check it against the one on my ID.

Once I got back to the studio, I set everything up and prayed for the plant right away. I like to use the prayer on the back of the Immaculate Heart of Mary holy card. It's a little too long, so I trimmed it a bit.

(She kneels on the small cushion and crosses herself.) In the name of the Father, and the Son, and the Holy Spirit. Amen.

"O MOST BLESSED MOTHER, heart of love, heart of mercy, ever listening, caring, consoling, hear this prayer:

Receive with understanding and compassion the petition placed before you today for this coleus, C40. Look after this plant, Blessed Mother, and keep it healthy and well. Respond to all its needs, as known through your Divine Wisdom.

I trust to your gentle care and intercession, this beloved plant when it is sick or alone or hurting. Help this plant to bear its burdens in this life until it may share eternal life and peace with God forever. Amen."

(Crossing herself)

In the name of the Father, and the Son, and the Holy Spirit. Amen.

Excerpt from *Vicarious Thrills*

CAROLYN GOELZER

Darkness. The sounds of traffic. There is the amplified sound of coins being dropped into a pay phone, then falling into the coin return box.

JANIS: Shit!

(The sound of more coins being inserted. A number is dialed on a rotary phone and begins ringing.)

Come on! Answer, answer, answer!

(Someone picks up the line. Lights up.)

Ummmm, yeah. I'd like to report a theft. Someone stole my dog. He was tied to a mailbox on Twenty-third and Grand. I went inside the building for a couple of minutes and when I come back out, he was gone! I don't know. I don't know, exactly . . . he's from a long line of "don't know who the father is"—you dig what I'm saying, honey? He's a nice dog, a really nice dog. He's part collie and part German shepherd. He's black and he's white, and he's got kind-of-a pointy . . . George. The name is George! Oh, uhhh . . . uhhh . . . Janis. Joplin. Yeah, Janis Joplin. Janis J-A-N-I-S J-O-P-L-I-N Joplin . . . I . . . I . . . Do I have to tell you? Because . . . because I'm famous, that's why! I don't want the cops or anyone else to . . . No, I just . . . wait. WAIT WAIT WAIT! Ma'am? I'll give you a number where I can be reached.

(She wipes the grime off the plastic that covers the number on the pay phone.)

It's . . . 784-9926. If you hear anything, will you call me right away? Call me right away. I'm just gonna wait here 'till you find him. Yeah, I'm . . . I'll just wait right here 'till you find him. God, I hope you find him. I'll kill that motherfucker who took him. I'm offering a reward. A cash re . . . Okay. Thanks a lot. Thank you, ma'am. Call me just as soon as . . .

(The sound of a receiver hanging up, then a dial tone. Janis sits dejectedly for a few moments, puts her head in her hands, cries. Time passes.)

Excerpt from *I'm Breathing the Water Now*

BASHORE HALOW

A hospice nurse in her forties defends her relationship to the black sheep of the town.

PATTY: Because I'm lonely, Mr. Riley! I'm lonely. Do you understand that? You had a wife. You had a good long marriage to her. What do I have? I'm in my forties. All I have to show for it is a tiny one-bedroom house, that I rent, that I don't even own for godsakes. I realize Ted is not Mr. Perfect. He is not a steady job holder. And yes he doesn't cut his hair and he is not the best . . . or the better or even a good boyfriend, but he is all I have. What do you think I'm made out of? How do you think it is possible for me to hold the hands of people who die and stay strong through that, to watch that and then go home . . . to that home . . . to that life? You've seen one death. I've seen too many to count. I sit there. I don't even help because I'm not called until all hope is gone. I just watch. Just . . . referee the last little bit. Afterwards everyone cries. It is not put on. It is genuine, rock bottom sadness. It is living a horrible, answerless truth. And then you know what I do? I get my coat, five years old now, and my shoulder bag and I get into my nine-year-old car, that hopefully starts, and I drive home where I sit in front of the TV and figure out something to have for dinner. So you'll forgive me if I admit to you that I enjoy the part of my night when I hear Ted's truck pull into my driveway. Or when I'm pushing the grocery cart down the aisle and picking out food that someone else likes. Or when I'm climbing into my bed and it is warm with the heat of someone else alive and alone like me. I make twenty-six thousand dollars a year. I have no retirement, no insurance. I have a job that I . . . don't really even know how I fell into. And I have a boyfriend. That's what I have. And so help me God, if you try to take him away from me, I'll never speak to you again.

Excerpt from *The Museum Play*

JORDAN HARRISON

Hallway

LUCY *is a museum guard. As she speaks to Jame, various exhibits sneak behind him: a plumed bird; a family of snakes; a wax Napoleon, stiffly. They are escaping. Every time Jame's attention drifts, every time he starts to look over his shoulder, Lucy's story seems to become more sensational.*

LUCY: First off Mother dropped me hard on the noggin right out of the starting gates then let me rot my teeth with too much sugar, rot my brain on the teletubby and stay out in the rain too long every night each and every without putting on my rubbers just to teach me a lesson never drink my milk while protecting me from all four basic food groups. Nothing in the house but a trough of candy corn. "One food group," she'd say, pointing. "Eat." Wash the candy down with Coca-Cola (never diet) and I was never to drive careful, she said, or take afternoon naps or play fair or share and by age two I was a pretty spectacular mess.

"Ruined her," Mother said. "Spoiled her with too much love." And she left me here, abandoned me over in the Egyptian wing, abandoned me in an authentic bulrush basket exhibit, Moses-like. Sense of humor on that woman. Funny like a Gila monster. And when Mr. Everly, the old Curator found me— "This baby isn't wax like the others!"—and taught me the difference between right and wrong, phylum and genus, Jurassic and Paleozoic—nursed me back to health in the great whirling cornucopia of the cafeteria, made me a feather bed of the stuff they stuff birds with and when I was legal age he put a walkie-talkie in my hand and set me to work, earn my keep and eventually I worked my way up to a spot on the Board of Directors on account of nobody else attends the meetings and—

I'm sorry, what was the question?

(Astonished silence. Jame: You were raised in the Museum?)

You shouldn't be angry with Mother. I wasn't. She visited every so often, on pay-what-you-wish nights. And on Christmas I'd round up my favorite playmates, the weasel and the dead-as-a dodo and the wildebeestie and we'd gather round the big evergreen in the lobby and oh what a celebration. Carols. I always got to be lead singer, to take the melody, and those were good years. Until Mr. Everly the old Curator ran out of breath one day very sudden, almost as if he was singing at notes inaudible to the human ear. *(Making soundless mouth movements)* Sort of mysterious. And when she came along to replace him the whole world turned oopsie-daisy.

Excerpt from *The Museum Play*

JORDAN HARRISON

Cabinet

The CURATOR delivers an acceptance speech. She cries crocodile tears, which gather on the floor in a champagne glass.

CURATOR: There are no words for it. You're too kind. I shall do my utmost to fill the humammoth shoes of the Head Curator position. I'm on cloud nine. Really I'm overwhelmed. Who would have thought a little girl from Minnesota would grow up to be the world's foremost authority? *Nobody* thought. There are a long list of naysayers, detractors, and ill-wishers who I really must take the time to mention.

> Winifred Chomps, at the Kineta Institute.
> Beauford Shaughnessy, rot in hell, at the Opal Center.
> The sewing circle at the Graduate School—worms eat your eyes for your words of discouragement.
> Rawley Pitkins.
> June Grimsley.
> Avril Pinch.
> Yolanda Mumford.
> I hope I haven't forgotten anyone.

And, of course, the friends and family who, with their words of encouragement, made all this possible:
(Awkward pause)
I hope I'm not forgetting anyone.

In conclusion, you really shouldn't have. Really you shouldn't. I'm touched beyond words—

I'm touched beyond—
I'm touched.
(She picks up the champagne glass, full of tears now, and holds it aloft in a toast.)
To the past!
(She drinks.)

Margaret Faydle Comes to Town from *Murderers*

JEFFREY HATCHER

I am a murderer. Well. Will be. Soon. That's a promise. Bob says I never stick to my guns, not even my figural guns, but then Bob's a stickler, and I'm not. His name's Bob Stickler, after all. My name's Stickler, too, but a Stickler by marriage is not the same thing. This time my gun's good and stuck.

It began when Margaret Faydle came to town. I should say Margaret Morrison Faydle Haverland Keith Sprechne Faydle Faydle. Which tells you something about Margaret's marital history. After her husbands would die or divorce her, she never ended up rich enough to take it easy. But she'd always end up on her feet, and in very nice shoes. I figured she couldn't always be in it for the money. Some of it must have been for . . . sport.

Hadn't seen her in a nun's age. And then one day . . . Margaret Faydle comes to town.

This was six weeks ago.

Standing at the corner outside the member's center next to Janet MacPherson and her new hip. I'd just come out of the pharmacy, with my pills and Bob's. What I see first is the hat. Ever since I knew her it was hats. When we were in school back home, it'd be some Saturday afternoon downtown, and there'd she be coming out of The Hub with something just in from Chicago or New York. She'd seen it on Rosalind Russell or Carole Lombard in some movie, and next thing you know it was on Margaret's head. Her father didn't have a lot of money either, he was strip steel manager at the mill, which is a good position, but it's not designed to keep a girl like Margaret in the manner to which she hopes to become accustomed. I think that family went without food to keep that bitch in hats.

Margaret wore hats all through the forties and fifties, like we all did, but when we stopped wearing them, she didn't. At first we thought that was strange or maybe she'd gone bald, but she knew better. It preserved her in the time the men she went after remembered as their best years—when a woman with a hat was just who they wanted and maybe couldn't quite get.

Standing outside the pharmacy with Janet MacPherson—who is not well by the way—I saw it. The hat. A sharp little flash of blue, at that angle. My heart skipped. I didn't want to look lower, but I had to. Below the blue hat, below the blue brim was the same pale brow and the pencil eyebrows and the red gash—Goddamnit Jesus Persnickety Christ!

I knew she wasn't visiting. Visitors go right through the main gates to whoever they're seeing. No, Margaret was walking into the offices of Mr. Finn and that nice Ms. Lupino. They show the units. And Margaret had luggage. That meant only one thing: Margaret Faydle was moving in. I tried not to show my true feelings. I didn't want Janet to know. And then I turned and looked at her. And Janet had gone white. And I knew then: Margaret had screwed Janet's husband, too.

Dinner at home that night. Bob and I are in one of the condos. The way things work at Riddle Key is . . . the biggest units are the Villas, they're detached, then the Condos, we share a garage with the Kilmers, from back home. Then the apartments. That's where you don't have more than a fridge and a zapper, and all your meals are down in the Coconut Room. Last is the senior center, the dump chute to death. I knew one couple, the Dahlbergs, who started at a Villa, then moved to a Condo, then an apartment, and ended in the center. Took 'em five years, start to stop. Fast and efficient. But then they liked those round the world in seventy-nine days tours, too.

Bob and I were watching *JEOPARDY!* Bob likes to play along, barking out, "I'll take Military Disasters for fifty!" I hadn't mentioned Margaret all day. Although the phone was ringing off the hook, and not just Janet MacPherson, every other woman in Riddle Key who had reason to remember or reason to fear. None of us were happy she was down here.

Last any of us had seen Margaret was back home at the club one summer right after she'd buried her last husband. I thought she might have come to the end of her time. She looked a little thinner—but then she was one of those gals who had one of those pillows that said "You can never be too rich or too thin" and she'd taken some of the stuffing out of the pillow to make it thinner.

Bob was barking next to me, "What was the Battle of the Bulge?!"

I turned to him.

"Janet MacPherson and I were down near the New Members Hut today after I picked up your pills and guess who we saw was moving in?"

The clue was "Winston Churchill said this famous line in Fulton, Missouri."

Bob didn't say a word. He squinted at the TV as if he was trying to think. Which is when I knew he knew Margaret was in town. He wasn't trying to answer the question, he was playing for time. I mean, even I knew the answer: this was a re-run.

"What is 'An Iron Curtain has descended'"?

* * *

That night, in bed, three in the morning, tossing and turning. It wasn't fair. Live seventy-eight years and you move all the way down to Florida to get away from the snow and cold, the bad memories, and then she has to come barging back in!

When I'd told Bob Margaret was moving in, he pretended to be surprised. Jesus, what a lousy actor! He even said, "Well, I'm very surprised!"

I didn't call him on it. Sometimes I think I've punished him enough. Twenty-seven years is probably enough.

Nah.

When it was new and raw, and they were going off to bonk like guppies in hotel rooms and her place and the back of the station wagon . . . and that one time they used our house when I was in the hospital with the hysterectomy—which irked me, I must confess . . . I was upset. And I was in no mood for forgiving, even after it was over, even after he said he'd called it off and realized his mistake and what could he do to make it up to me . . . hands clasped like Mary Pickford, on his knees in the rec room, his bad knees as he reminded me through his tears . . . only time I ever saw Bob cry was that night and the day I wrecked the Crown Victoria.

He said he'd ended it, and he was wrong and a fool and not worth my love . . . and would I take him back . . . ?

I did. I made it hard on him, of course. Weeks of silence and coolness. Thaw bit by bit, and then, when he thought he was safe and on firm footing, hit him with it again. Sometimes it was planned. Sometimes it just bubbled up. I could always count on it bubbling up.

Of course I had believed him, believed him when I found out they were at the motel that last afternoon, May 9, 1975, that he had gone there to call it off of his own volition, instead of the truth which was that she told him to meet her there so she could tell him she was dumping him to marry Lou Sprechne.

And I had to pretend he had chosen to come back to me.

Well, what do you do when you're forty-nine years old, no children, living in a mock colonial near the lake?

I punished him. For a few years. We tried to avoid her at parties and places, but it's a small town, and frankly when you realize your husband is one of a team, it starts to get almost funny. The rest of us began to pick out the signs when Margaret was about to swoop onto one of the other husbands. Sometimes we'd try to warn the wronged wife, discreet little warnings like "Margaret is fucking your husband."

By the time we hit sixty, things had teetered back to normal . . . by which I mean I was apologizing to Bob for not making dinner on time, and not having his shirts pressed correctly, and not picking up the pills, and not being interesting enough to require his love or devotion and fidelity.

And this is how things were for us that night, at three A.M. the day Margaret Faydle came to Riddle Key. Me awake in the bed, wondering why my life had come to this.

And Bob awake next to me . . . wondering what, I wondered.

* * *

The invitation came the next day. Cocktails at six. A welcoming party for Margaret Faydle thrown by . . . Margaret Faydle.

I was at Dr. Nagangupta's office to get the results of my tests, and Janet had all the dirt:

Margaret was staying in Ted Varner's villa just six circles away. Ted and Sheila Varner had lived there until Sheila died last spring and then when Ted broke his back coming out of the Tiki Hut six weeks ago they'd moved him straight to the senior center, but he hadn't given up his villa. Ted's certain he's going to move back, but everybody knows no one comes back from the senior center.

Apparently Margaret heard the villa was empty and called Ted, said she was looking for a place to stay the winter, boohoo, and one-two-three, here she is. And now she's throwing her own welcoming party, using Ted's charge cards, Janet says.

And we're invited. Well, everybody's invited. Not just the men she slept with and the women she ruined.

I go into Dr. Nagangupta's to talk about the tests, the follow-up, the new prescriptions, the second and third opinions. Dr. Nagangupta was sued once for malpractice—a woman had come in with a toe infection and ended up having her earlobes removed—so now he's obsessed with being thorough while at the same time being completely noncommittal. When he's done, he shows me pictures of his kids—he's very proud.

I'm supposed to take my X-rays into St. Petersburg to see the new specialist, but I stop when I see her. My hand on the handle of the car, there she is, in a golf cart—she doesn't golf, everyone has golf carts down here—Margaret, whizzing by with a hat on at a jaunty angle, a cigarette stabbing up into the air like a sex change Roosevelt.

And Bob in the seat next to her. His golf hat blows off. Bob makes a grab for it, but it's gone. Margaret laughs. They both laugh. And the golf cart zooms off through a row of forsythia.

That night. Dinner.

Bob's late. He was going to have lunch at the club then play cards at the Stag Room he said. I would be home from St. Petersburg by five to make dinner.

It's six when he comes in. He kisses me on the forehead, sits close, on the ottoman, how was the doctor, what did he say? I say fine. His bald head is burned. His bald head, which has made him fear skin cancer since the age of thirty-six. His bald head, on which he smears three kinds of sunscreen with an SPF of 198, this before he puts on his hat, is burnt to a crisp.

"You're red," I say.

"A little," Bob says. He is sanguine about his peeling, red head and the carcinoma that is steadily brightening over his shining pate.

"Where's your hat?"

"Lost it."

Bob is relaxed about the loss of his hat, his favorite hat, the hat he got when he and the fellas won the Riddle Skins Senior two years before. Bob gets angry if he loses a pack of matches from the Winn-Dixie, but today he could care less if he lost his favorite first place trophy hat.

I show him the invitation. His brow furrows, red and white grooves as he pretends not to know about the cocktail party.

"Should we go?" he asks. "It's up to you," he says. "Would you be comfortable?" He takes my hand, he's very solicitous, he's like Marcus Welby.

I say no.

He nods. Nods again. He wants to go, the bastard.

"Okay," he says. "We won't. We'll be the only ones though. That'll stick out."

Bob goes into the kitchen to take his pills.

JEOPARDY! is on. "Famous Murderers for forty." "Gave him forty whacks."

"All right," I call to him. "We'll go. But we won't stay long."

Bob is ecstatic. But he shakes his head.

"No, really, if it's uncomfortable, if it makes you feel inhibited or shy . . ."

Note the problem: it's not that she stole my husband from me then threw him back like a dead fish, it's that I'm too shy and inhibited by her blazing light to be in the room with her.

"No," I say. "We're going."

Bob sighs, pops a beta blocker. "If you say so."

Tom Sawyer thinks he's made the dumb girl paint another fence.

And all the time I know his golf hat is under the cushion of my La-Z-Boy.

* * *

Night of the cocktail party. For the last three days every married woman in Riddle Key has spent her every waking hour in front of mirrors—mirrors at the dress shop, mirrors at the make-up table, mirrors in the car on the way to the party. Like the German army, Margaret Faydle makes her opponents rise to the occasion.

We pull into Ted's circle. Lots of golf carts. We still drive a car, but pretty much everyone else is using golf carts now. Margaret has hired some valet boys. They use cars to drive them to where they park the golf carts.

I wave at the boys. The boys love me.

"Hola, Senora Stickler!"

The Villa is filled. Everybody from back home is there. That's one of the strangest things you learn when you retire to Florida. You all move down in a group. The same people you lived near when you were starting out and the kids were at school, the same people you had barbecues with and drunken kisses behind the bar are still just down the lane, only now we're tanned like rawhide and can't remember our names.

I don't see Margaret when I come in. I get a drink. A Brandy Alexander without the brandy. I like the brandy, but the brandy does not like me.

Bob disappeared the moment we came in the door. Janet says it's some law of physics, that the moment a couple enters a party, the husband and wife are immediately sucked into two different parts of the room.

I roam through the place, looking at Ted's things. Any evidence that Sheila ever lived there is gone. Ted said it was just too hard for him to look at things that reminded him of her, but everyone knew he was just using that as an excuse to get rid of the stuff he'd always hated, like the little bear collection and the pink sea shell shelves. The death of a spouse gives you a lot of leeway to clear out the crap.

I go through the den to the deck . . .

And there she is. At a table near the balcony, seated, with the man-made marsh and the sun behind her, surrounded by as many men as are alive and ambulatory.

Bob stands apart, holding a martini—neither Bob nor I drink martinis. Bob has a look on his face as he watches Margaret with her other beaus. It's a look I've never seen on Bob before but I recognize it. I've seen it in movies, on TV shows, I've seen it in my own face many years before but never on Bob. It's jealousy.

We don't talk about it during the drive home, the three minutes' drive home that we could have walked when we were young and he first betrayed me. We don't talk about it that night. Or the next morning or for the next three weeks.

And then, it's a Tuesday, I've made my trip to the pharmacist's to get Bob's Lexapro and his mineral ice. Bob is supposed to drive me into St. Petersburg for the test results. But when I get back to the house, he says his back is killing him. Can Janet drive me. I can drive myself, so I say yes. Relax.

In St. Petersburg, in the doctor's office, I wait. There are two gals across the coffee table from me. I don't know them, but I've seen their faces. They live over at Sunset Point. I pretend to leaf through an AARP brochure. They're talking about someone.

"They say she moved down when she got wind one of her old beaus has a wife who's on her last legs, and she's just waiting for the day she kicks it."

I don't wait for my results.

I get into the car and drive back to Riddle Key. I drive too fast. I run a red light. Someone shouts at me. In Spanish.

I want to see Bob. The Bob I met my first summer back from college, who I gave up my dreams of being the first female pharmacist in town for! The Bob who woo'd me, loved me, stood with me in front of God and my family and my friends and made promises to last a lifetime.

I'm home a good two hours sooner than I'd expected. Or he'd expected. Because Bob isn't home nursing his back.

I go down to the drug store to get my Valium—I'm having palpitations and as I'm about to leave, the druggist, the snarky one, the one who looks like a weasel, says—

"Uh-oh. One more."

He turns and fishes around for a bottle.

"Just got the call. Lucky you came by."

He hands me the bottle and smiles a greasy grin.

"Have a good night."

And he winks at me.

I go out into the sun. Into the car, up the drive, three circles to our house, inside and into my bathroom and I open the bottle.

The name: Robert Stickler. The prescription: Viagra . . .

* * *

I began planning the murder the next day.

I went to the pharmacist first. Andrew, the young one. He's so sweet. And confused. I tell him the prescription I got the day before didn't have my Vallorturinal in it. He seems surprised, but he believes me, and he refills it.

When he goes to lunch, I go back and see Misty, the one with the funny eye. The prescription I got from Andrew didn't have my Vallorturinal. She's an idiot, so she believes me, too.

I do the same thing at the St. Petersburg Eckerd's and the Clearwater Rexall, three times each. By the end of the day I have enough Vallorturinal to kill everyone in the state of Florida.

I go home. It's *JEOPARDY!* time. But Bob is out. Bob is out all the time now. He's volunteering, he says. He's a Big Brother or a Fat Grandpa or whatever the hell he's pretending to be. But I know he's slipping from yard to yard until he gets to Margaret's villa.

He has hidden his Viagra. He puts it in his golf bag, down in the sack where he keeps his balls. Two pills a day. I switch them for Ex-Lax.

When I retrieve the mail that day I see there's a dance at the club Saturday night. Saturday. Saturday will be perfect.

As I said, I always wanted to be a pharmacist, and even now I always study the backs of my prescriptions. I know what to take on an empty stomach, what to take with food, how much water, and not to drive a tractor when I'm doing it.

The Bob part will be easy. We share a medicine cabinet.

But Margaret will be difficult.

For the next three days I'm on a tight schedule.

Wednesday I go in for my weekly appointment with Dr. Nagangupta. We do what we do, check the tests, sigh at the results. When it's nearly done, I ask him, "And how are those kids of yours?" He beams. He turns and digs out his wallet—he never can resist—and while he's looking away for just an instant, I peel off three of his prescription sheets from his pad and pocket them before he faces me again.

That afternoon, when Bob's back from another bout of his newfound social conscience, he finds me in bed. I tell him I need my pills, but I forgot to get my prescription filled, can he go down to the pharmacy.

Usually Bob would berate me for being so unorganized, but the trip will give him a chance to drop by Margaret's. So he says yes. I give him the prescriptions: three of them—my forgeries of Dr. Nagangupta's signature on every one.

Thursday I go into St. Petersburg with Janet to buy a dress. It costs three thousand dollars of Bob's money. And it's worth it. Janet is amazed. She buys a muumuu sort of thing. Janet has been buying muumuus since she was forty.

Back home, I check to see if Bob is watching TV. No. He's left me a note. He's doing craft work with some underprivileged Seminole kids.

It's Friday, the day before the dance. I call Margaret Faydle.

"Hullo?" That fake English accent she stole from Greer Garson in *Mrs. Miniver.*

"Margaret?"

A pause. She knows my voice.

"Why, Lucy. I'm so sorry we didn't get a chance to chat the other night!"

"Me, too!" I say in my sparky housewife voice. We gals know how to make up for our lack of innate interest by over-compensating in the Doris Day department.

"That's why I was wondering. What if I dropped over tomorrow noon!"

Another pause.

"Why, that would be swell," Margaret coos. She uses words like swell and nifty. The sporty old slut. "It'll be neat to catch up!"

The next morning, I'm up early. Bob is in, watching The History Channel. *Great Traitors.*

"Not out with the NAACP today, dear? No street kids to teach English to?"

"Er . . . no. They're, uh, they're under house arrest for the weekend."

He's so good at lying. He knows I'm having lunch with Margaret, so he's got nowhere to go.

I put on another new outfit I've bought. Eight hundred smackers this time.

I say goodbye to Bob. He doesn't notice the outfit. He's entranced by the voice of Roger Mudd and the face of Alger Hiss.

I take the car to the Varner Villa.

When Margaret opens the door, I am amazed. She is a sight. A 1950s thing, all camel and cream. And yet it's not out of style. Nothing on Margaret ever goes out of style.

"My dear one!" Peck peck, each cheek. "Do, do, come in."

And I do.

It's quiet when she shuts the door. Just the sound of the sun outside. The hum of the air conditioner.

"Here," she purrs, "come through. Drink—Drink? Or can't you?"

"Why can't I?"

"Well . . . I thought . . . or someone said . . . someone mentioned . . ."

Bob has said, Bob has mentioned.

"I can have a Brandy Alexander with just a little brandy."

"Brandy Alexander. Such a little lady!"

"What're you having?" I ask.

"Gin with a scotch chaser."

"Make it two."

Margaret's eyes widen. I recall she was the first gal back home to wear contact lenses. Half the wives she cuckolded found out they were being cheated on when they found her little round glass things in their husband's boxer shorts.

When we've sat down—she's made mine a triple, to see if I'll throw up—we talk about the dance that night.

"Yes, I'm going," says Margaret. "Of course."

"Not alone!"

"Oh, my dear, no. There's a perfectly charming little Cuban developer I met at lunch the other day. He wants to show me his bodega."

The time has come. I stand.

"What's the matter, dear? Drink too strong?"

I have been careful with the drink. But I pretend otherwise.

"I should have checked my medication. May I use your powder room?"

"Of course, petal."

And I run to the hall. Run, so she will be discouraged from following me.

As I pass the bedroom, I take out Bob's Senior Skins hat and toss the hat under the bed with one swift swish, like I'm Oddjob from *Goldfinger*.

I go into the bathroom. I run the water. I've only got a minute or two before she comes knocking to see if my head's in the toilet.

I open her medicine cabinet. Margaret doesn't have the kind of medications I have. Just four rows of diet pills. I only need one. I choose it, careful not to smear her prints. I empty the pills into the toilet, peel off the prescription label and throw it in the toilet too. The clock ticks, quickly, quickly, nimble Lucy, do the switches!

The rattle of pills in bottles, the shake-a-shake-a sound. Water running, sweat running.

"How are we doing, Dear?"

I put Margaret's bottle into my purse, flush the toilet, take off my watch and drop it under the paper roll.

I open the door.

All done.

I say I'd better be going, lie down for a while before the dance. She does not try to stop me.

As I leave the villa, I break down and cry. The tears are real, although I hadn't intended them to be.

The Cuban gardeners see me, take it in, try not to notice. And then, when I am sure, I have my witnesses, I get into my car and go home. I make sure no one sees while I drop the spare key in the flower pot. I go inside and lock the door.

The phone is ringing. Margaret has found the watch.

"Dear one, you silly, you left your absolutely charming timepiece in my powder room. Shall I bring it to the dance tonight?"

"Oh, dear," I say, "Would—Would you mind bringing it over to the house?"

"Now?"

"Do you mind too terribly?"

I can hear the furious sigh, but she says yes.

"If I'm in the bath, come in the side door, there's a key in the flower pot."

She's on her way! As Margaret pulls her golf cart into the driveway I call Janet across the street. I whisper, like I'm hiding in the closet.

"Janet, someone's trying to get into my house!"

"Lemme see," she grumbles. I see Janet lumber to her front window and stare across the street. "It's goddamn Margaret Faydle."

"What?"

"She's taking some key from the flower pot."

"Why, I don't leave a key in the flower pot!"

"Well, she's inside now, so you better get ready to hit her with a frying pan."

I click off. I hear Margaret slap down the watch on the kitchen counter, and leave.

* * *

I take a bath, a long one, the oils and salts. I take a long time dressing, my make up, my hair.

When I pass his room, Bob is struggling into his tux. Actually it's not so much a struggle anymore. He's lost weight. He's

113

keeping fit. All that basketball he's playing with the Special Olympics team.

I look at myself in the mirror. One last time.

We drive together to the club.

Inside, Bob looks over my shoulder to see her, no doubt.

I go to the bar where Dr. Nagangupta is standing.

"And how are you doing tonight, Mrs. Stickler?"

"I'm a little woozy tonight. All those pills Bob said you want me to take."

"Woozy?" He looks perplexed.

"The pills Bob said you prescribed. You sure do have me taking a ton of them!"

Dr. Nagangupta furrows his brow. "But I have not prescribed a ton of—"

"Oh! Excuse me," I say, and move away from the good and honest doctor, leaving him with his perplexing thought.

In a corner, Janet is nursing a vat of vodka.

"Hey, how'd things go with Margaret?"

"Well, she seemed very surprised when I came out of the bedroom. She said she wanted to drop off something, but when I pressed her she couldn't tell me what it was."

"What about the key?"

"Well, I asked her how she got in and she said the door was unlocked."

"Lying bitch. I saw her take the key. Well, if you didn't leave the key, who did?"

And I leave Janet, my faithful friend with the dark suspicion that will linger in her mind.

I go to Bob. He's watching Margaret with her Cuban, a short little Baptista tanned the color of a coffee table. Bob's watching them but he's pretending to talk wetlands policy with Mort Hoberman. Mort is pro wetlands, Bob is for a state made of asphalt.

"Bob. I'm . . . I'm not doing too good."

"What is it?"

"I don't know, I . . . could you take me home?"

Bob goes red. He has just seen an entire evening of thermometers and cold compresses flash before him.

"You don't have to stay with me. Just get me home, and you can come back."

"No, honey, I should stay with you."

Note the "should."

"Just take me home."

And we leave.

At home, I assure my husband of forty-seven years that I feel better. That it was just the heat and the crowd and my condition, which, as Dr. Nagangupta and the specialists have said, doesn't get better, I remind him.

Bob smiles down on me with a look of what looks like love and sympathy. Then he steals a glance at his watch.

"Go back to the dance, dear. Have fun."

Bob leans in, pecks my cheek.

And he's gone.

It's very quiet now. Not even the sound of the grass. I sit at my dressing table. I take the pill bottle I stole from Margaret's medicine cabinet and stick one of my little Vallorturinal labels on it. And then I open the pill bottles. There are nine of them. A lot to take. But I have plenty of water.

After I'm done, I will put the empty pill bottles in the trash.

And when they find my body late that night they will think it was by natural causes. I was very ill, after all, everyone knew that. But they thought I had more time.

And then Dr. Nagangupta will remember what I said about Bob giving me more pills than he had prescribed. And fearing a wrongful death suit, he will order an autopsy, where they'll find my stomach full of poison.

And then the pharmacy will retrieve the forged prescription slips written with Bob's pen and taken in by Bob not long before I died.

And the pill bottles will be found. One of them with Margaret's fingerprints on them—the bottle I took from her own medicine cabinet.

And Janet will recall Margaret sneaking into my house with a key left there by someone who was not me.

And Bob's hat will be found under Margaret's bed.

And the gardeners will recall my weeping.

And they will be arrested for my murder. And in this state, they will fry.

So. I am a murderer. Will be. Soon as the pills take hold.

Oh, I know they might not get the chair. Old people, after all. But old people go fast in prison. Bob becoming the bitch of a three-time loser named Baby Lard. And Margaret taking showers with all those "nice girls" in the diesel joint.

It's not perfect justice. But then . . . I'm not a stickler.

Excerpt from *Across the Desert*

CORY HINKLE

NATALIE: She says to me my friend, my pal, my *confidante*, she says, "Natalie! What's wrong with you? Why are you so obsessive?" I say, "Obsessive? I'm not obsessive." It's just that I think (and I believe I'm right on this) that I should and will and *must* get what I want like everybody, like all human beings and what I want is *this guy*. What's wrong with that? She says, "What's wrong is that people shit on you over and over again and you keep coming back for more." So, let me tell you what's wrong with this whole situation. You see, my friend, my pal she's so *strong*, she's such a *feminist* or whatever but the only, *only* reason she's never been shit on before, as she so wonderfully puts it, is because she's never, once in her mediocre and mundane life, she's never put herself in the *position* to be shit on because yes, in order to get to that point you must love and sometimes the results suck. It hurts, it makes me not want to move, makes me want to crawl back into bed like it's a womb and I'm not coming out, I'm not coming out into the light of day, but I do. I come back because I will never, ever give up on this feeling because I know it's real and you can call me obsessive and crazy and you can say, "Natalie, there are so many fish in the sea, what's so important about this one?" But, I can't explain this to you. It's all a crazy madness, this crazy-mad feeling that I get from him and yeah, he's got problems, he's definitely got some hang-ups but I see us working past all that and for us to do that, to work past his hang-ups, I have to master my own destiny and that may mean pushing and shoving and thrashing and it may mean explosive blow-ups in public places and somebody might get hurt but I will get what I want. I will get this love. Love. *Love.*

A Walk on Lake Superior from *Tabloid Tales*

EUGENIA JENSEN

RITA, an attractive woman of about sixty, sits next to a hospital bed. There is the beep-beep of a heart monitor. Rita has a laptop computer in front of her.

RITA: I can't believe what they're selling these days. Like there aren't enough garage sales and want ads, we've got this eBay as a twenty-four-hour flea market. You can sell anything here, lucky for us. Oh, my God, I can't believe it! I swear, right here in front of me is that cocktail set we used to use. Same tall glasses printed with W. C. Fields in black and "Who took the cork out of my lunch" printed in silver. I got those from your mother when she got the new set that had those funny golfers on them. Remember those? Boy, I couldn't wait until she filled those up those long Sunday afternoons waiting for your father to get off the course so we could have dinner. And by that time, it didn't matter what she served. I'll tell you, tongue doesn't taste as bad as you'd think as long as you have a nice, fresh Manhattan to wash it down with. And look, they even have the handy, dandy decorative rack that holds all eight glasses and a pitcher for the cocktails in case you want to move to another room. I always felt so smart when I used them, so sophisticated as we served . . . what was that new drink that year? Oh, yeah. Rum Runners. Such a pretty color and tasted like Hawaiian Punch. After a few pitchers of those I'm sure the Joneses, Sandersons, and Richmans didn't care what we served either. Remember that one night when I forgot to serve dinner at all? Got up the next morning and there was the Crock-Pot still full of those Tulip

Surprise meatballs. The secret ingredient was a small jar of grape jelly and half cup of Coca-Cola.

Let's see what's going on with our stuff. Wow. Up to $2,000 on that one and this one is $16,000 . . . and someone will pay $15 for each nail. Never thought about selling those, but $15 is $15. That would be . . . times ten . . . no twenty . . . three hundred bucks.

(She hits a few keys.)

The jewelry isn't doing so well. They haven't even bid on that necklace you told me belonged to Angie Dickinson. I knew it didn't, but I knew how much you liked Angie Dickinson. So I let you believe that I believed you. You used to get so hot and bothered when I put it on, just thinking that that necklace might have touched her neck, so close to those breasts that had been breathed on by every member of the Rat Pack. You always liked breasts . . . and the Rat Pack. That one night we were late for dinner with the Richmans because you couldn't keep your hands off me. I was kind of insulted. Remember? I hardly talked to you all night. I was on that crazy diet and I would have killed for a bite of that creamy, cheesy lobster you'd ordered. But I thought if you liked Angie Dickinson better than me . . . I know now you didn't. It was just an idea. A fantasy in the blip in the connection between you loving me and some primal need for you to have every woman in the world panting for you. I understood when I went through my Charles Bronson phase. But I think you should know that she's put on quite a bit of weight and I don't think she's really keeping up the old hair color. Angie Dickinson. Kind of sounds like the name of a porn star.

Almost 3:00. Better check the investments. Only a few minutes left on this one. Oh my God, the price is up to $40,000! Going . . . going . . . gone! $43,200! Who would have ever even thought!

I haven't told anyone how I'm selling things off. They wouldn't understand. Heck, even I think it's kind of creepy sometimes. But they're all things that you won't be using. My God, I wish you could! If only you'd listened to me all those years of Camel straights, Lobster Thermidor, and Manhattans maybe you wouldn't be lying there going beep-beep-beep. You're younger than me, for God's sake! This shouldn't have happened, and here I am selling bits and pieces of your life. Our life. I know I should be thankful for the years we had, grateful the doctors have given me these extra three days with you so I can get you . . . your affairs tied up . . . but there should have been more. Just one more walk on Lake Superior.

I'll tell you who wouldn't understand this. Janet. How did the two of us get such a straight arrow daughter? Corporate lawyer at twenty-six, judge by thirty-five. She decides people's fate all day long. I suppose it would only be natural for her to condemn or laud me, too. But I don't think she'll hand me any laurel crowns for this. She does love you. She's sent flowers every week. A tape of all those songs you used to sing to her. But this . . . well, it's none of her business. These are all private transactions. And even though these things may be a bit worn, they may do someone some good for a few years. And the money that you left her is perfectly safe, just waiting to be transferred to her name. It's our dreams that have been under-funded.

Andrew? I'm sorry about my hair. Really, really sorry. Every week at the beauty shop, standing appointment at 1:00. The only thing that ever interrupted it was your mother having that kidney stone attack. She couldn't have waited two hours, could she? They'd wash my hair, and set it, and then I'd sit under the dryer reading the *Enquirer*. I have to admit, the dryer felt good. All that warm air rushing over my skull, relaxing the muscles that hold my hair . . . reading about Burt and Dinah, and Farrah, and Elvis. And good, old "Miss Connie is it too hot? How does that feel? Can I get you a Pepsi-Lite?" After a week of washing and ironing and cooking and cleaning it was like a mini vacation. And then they'd fluff my hair and lacquer it down with Aqua Net. The city dump must be half full of cans of that stuff. I probably have brain damage from the fumes. But

I'd tie a red silk scarf over my new hair, and saunter confidently out to the Cadillac. And then I'd be imprisoned for the week. Wouldn't comb it for two days, slept with toilet paper wrapped around my head . . . no wonder you dreamed about Angie! I stayed out of all weather. I missed all those lovely walks on vacation at Lake Superior with you and Janet because I didn't want the wind to wreck my hair. Remember the one time I did walk with you? The infinite expanse of water in front of me was the shade of blue the sky turns for a moment just after the sun sets. The waves hitting those huge craggy boulders and exploding into shards, then rushing back out and sucking more water with them, then coming back again. Then that one wave that came crashing in four feet farther than any of the others hitting me like liquid ice, dripping down my green silk sweater. You and Janet laughed and I was so mad. I stomped back to the car and refused to go out to dinner until I found a beauty shop to re-do my hair. I never went swimming, or out in the rain or snow. *(Beat)* I don't have my hair done anymore. I walk wherever and whenever I want and if I end up looking like a German shepherd, I don't give a damn. I do kind of miss the dryer. Maybe I can find one on eBay. Set it up right in the living room and instead of getting a massage, I'll just heat my head.

There's a doctor over there looking in. He's trying to be subtle, polite, but I know they want to get this over with. He looks about twelve. But he's been a good doctor. Very respectful . . . explained that even though your organs still work, still keep the blood pumping, you went too long without oxygen after the stroke. My CPR didn't work. I tried, Andrew. You know I did. But now your brain doesn't work. There's so much locked up in there and it can't get out. All those stories, poems, songs, and pain. And the pain is locked up in your heart. I hope the man . . . or woman who bought it gets your compassion and grace. The person who bought your lungs got a discount because you smoked for so long. But they'll give him a few more years, I hope. Oh, he's waving at me. It must be time. There's only a small window of time between disconnecting you and harvesting your

121

organs. I really find that term odd. Harvesting an organ. I mean, you harvest grain, you harvest hay, you have a harvest party barn dance. There really should be a more dignified word for this. He's coming over now. Okay, my darling. I'll be here. I'll watch your spirit fly from your body and into the great beyond. Wait for me. It probably won't be that long. I'll look for you. I'll wear the necklace. I'm going to write it into my will that I'm to be buried in it. I guess it's time. *(She looks at him as if he'd spoken.)* No, sweetheart. I didn't sell that one. That one belongs to me alone.

Excerpt from *The Love Song of J. Robert Oppenheimer*

CARSON KREITZER

LILITH: I've heard all this sssssssomewhere before.
God says
I've got this great idea
I'm going to make a woman
out of dirt
and breathe into her nostrils and look how beautiful
SHE LIVES.

Adam and Lilith, my playthings. I breathed my wet god-breath into their little dirt mouths and look at the mud things walking around naming the beasts, eating the plants.

Then Adam says to me LIE DOWN
as if we were not both the same
he says LIE DOWN I WANT TO
and I say, hey, wait a minute here, I'm not saying let's not have fun, but what makes you the one to climb up on top of me? I don't think this is really about sex here I don't think this is about exploring these new bodies with the new wet life breathed in I think this is about you trying to get on top of me
LIE DOWN
I think you want to hold me there
LIE DOWN
He would not stop saying it and his face all red
LIE DOWN
Grabbed both my arms and tried to knock me down in the dirt we'd both come from.

I spoke the sacred name of God and flew up into the sky.

Went off on my own, to the shores of the red sea. 'Till he
thought better of his behavior.
We're all learning here, after all.

But Adam
Adam goes to God and he complains
that I will not lie down and God says

What?

Don't worry, little man
I will make you a new one.

I will rip open your side

and take from you

since you would not take what I made you the first time

(and I thought, made You?)

let me rip a piece from you
close to the heart

now I take this dripping bloody piece of you and I make you a
woman who will lie down.
She will do nothing but lie down.
She will lie down for you.

And to me he says
eat their babies.
They are delicious.

Especially the red-brown marrow in the troughs of their white
bones.

Excerpt from *Mallbaby*

JENNIFER MAISEL

MAGGIE, five months pregnant and fearing she's lost the baby, confronts her doctor. Maggie is a reporter on the mall beat at US Mall, a mall slowly taking over the country.

MAGGIE: First we thought it was the normal hard time conceiving—everyone keeps telling you to relax or it'll happen when you stop thinking about it but when you try to stop thinking about something you've just added a whole new level of thinking about it, a layer of trying to dismiss or thinking you have to stop thinking of thoughts running through your head that you haven't stopped thinking and you're doing it all wrong and it's your fault because you're so tense and relax, damnit, relax.

So we did all the testing at Dr. Baum's before the insurance switched me here—I'm sure it's there in my chart—and Mark passed with flying colors and we did the whole test tube thing which made me think—What do you tell your kids about the night they were conceived—do you maybe have a pamphlet about that somewhere? Because I can't seem to come up with a plausible romantic memory about weeks of fertility shots and my legs up in stirrups as a way to start this whole damn thing as well as finishing—a pamphlet would be a good idea, don't you think? And then I realize it doesn't matter very much because the miracle of life is manifesting itself in the very clichéd throwing up and sleeping all the time ways, so it's a done thing and my kid will just have to deal with the fact that his parents didn't have sex to make him, Dr. Freud.

And while Mark might think it's cute, I'm not finding any of this pregnancy thing romantic and I don't believe in any fucking glow that's for sure and I look fat, I look really fat which bugs me because we haven't told anyone yet so I can tell in their eyes they think I'm not going to the gym anymore which I'm not doing, actually, because I'm too busy sleeping and throwing up but still.

And my breasts have gotten really big which Mark likes and I like and the fat is now obviously enlarged uterus and the ultrasound—the heartbeat—and I know I am mother potential on the brink.

Saturday morning I woke up and I felt different—just different. My breasts—I mean the cleavage was gone and I didn't need the saltines for the first time in weeks and I felt disconnected unplugged somehow—un . . . Mark tried to jolly me out of it and he convinced me of my very own paranoia and the consequences of raging hormones but I kept saying, that's it, my hormones aren't raging, are not stampeding, aren't controlling. They have been subdued.

I called the service. I left a message—Saturday night, I bet you doctors love that. Is this an emergency? An emergency implies something that has to be taken care of right away. Something that action can determine the outcome of like this—which has not been decided. So yes . . . yes this is an emergency. An emergency implies . . .

I went to Your Future Is Ours To See on the third level and she gave me this affirmation and a little crystal to promote my fertility. My body is the perfect home for my child. My body is the perfect home for my child. My body is the perfect home for my child. But it doesn't seem . . . I can't . . . I want to . . .

I don't think we ever thought a baby would be something we'd have to work for.

We tried so hard.

Wide Open

MELANIE MARNICH

JULIA, a woman in her mid-fifties.

Pitch dark.
A camera flash illuminates a nude woman.
Darkness.
Another flash.
Darkness.
Flash.
Flash.
Flash.

Darkness.

Lights up on Julia.

JULIA: How many eyes are on you?
Can they see you in the dark?
Can they see through your walls?
Through your clothes?
Through your hands when you touch between your legs?
Do you blush?
Do they blink?
Do they ever turn away?
Ever turn you on?
Are they everywhere you go?
Can they see everything you do?
Do you care?

I was brought up to believe that when our loved ones died, they
didn't really go away. They just ascended into heaven where they

could watch over us, day and night, and we could take comfort in their gaze.

This sounds great in theory. It might even be romantic.
But it's not sexy.
Even alone in my bed, when my hand would start to go down on my body,
I would look up.
I could see through the ceiling, past the trees and the stars, right into bright heaven.
And there they were.
Four grandparents, two great aunts, one not-so-great uncle, a cousin, two cats, a dog, and a hamster named Penny.
Looking. At me.
Shame
Shame
Shame.

So.
Sleep with pajamas on.
Fuck with the lights off.
Never relax.
Never release.
Never let go.
No matter how much you need it.
How much you want it.
You ache and crave and shiver
But you just can't.

The ad was for a photography class.
At night. At the university.
I ripped it out.
I called.
I went.
I was the oldest person there.

I took nice pictures of apples and of people waiting for the bus
and of old buildings.
The final project was to take a self-portrait.

She was, I'd guess, about thirty years old.
She said her final project was going to be me.
A portrait of me.
I said it's supposed to be a *self*-portrait.
She said she didn't follow instructions very well.

She had her own small studio in her apartment.
Some cameras, a tripod.
A couple of lights.

She touched my clothes—
"You'll want to take these off," she said.
"It's okay. We're doing art."

She posed me.
First my chin—
"Look this way."
My arm—
"Like this."
My back—
"Turn, bend."
My belly—
"Soft. Soft."
My thighs—
"Relax."
My feet—
"Just . . . there."

She laid the photos on the floor.
"You're beautiful," she said.
I didn't breathe.

"You have no idea," she said.
Couldn't breathe.

She took my hand and placed it on the picture of my face.
"Can you feel this?"

    (Julia's not sure.)

She moved my fingers down my black-and-white throat to my
black-and-white nipples.
"How about this?"

    (Julia nods a soft "yes.")

Down to my belly, between my legs—
"And this?"

    (Julia nods an excited "yes.")

She laid me down on the floor next to the photos.
This time, without words, without pictures.
Her hands on my hands on my body.
Face
Neck
Shoulders
Breasts
Nipples nipples
A long time spent on nipples.
A longer time spent further down.
Longer.
More.

And then, right then,
Naked on my back on the floor
In the arms of a woman nearly half my age

I looked up and I could see through the ceiling.
Through the trees.
The clouds parted as the sun made way
as the sky cracked open as I sang—
Look at me.
Look.
This
Is
Beautiful.

(Lights fade on Julia and quickly come up on her photo image—a life-size portrait of her, nude, made up of separate photos pieced together like a mosaic.
Her face turned and blurred in pleasure.
Her neck and breasts.
Belly.
Lower belly to upper thighs.
Legs.
Feet.
The lights slowly fade.)

That's What It Means to Have a Duke Heart from *Hazard County*

ALLISON MOORE

JESSICA, twenty, Canadian. She wears casual, inexpensive clothes. She swears a little awkwardly at first.

JESSICA: You know they're taking it off the air? Well, I mean again, you know, off the cable. The bastards! It just happened. I signed the petition about a million times, we all did. But I know it's just temporary, they have to bring it back. I mean, we're too devoted, the fans? And there are a lot more *Dukes of Hazzard* fans than regular people think, even here. Some people try to make it sound like it's weird that I'm such a huge fan. Like you can only be a fan if you're from Georgia or something, or really into cars? They used to leave nasty postings on my message board and all that. But anyone who looks at the site figures out that my heart is true, you know? Doesn't matter if I'm from Manitoba, I have a Duke heart. So then they keep coming back, to my Hazzard online. Well, unless they're creeps just looking for nude pictures of Catherine, because I don't have anything like that. And I say Catherine, because Daisy would never pose nude, she's a virgin? And besides, Uncle Jesse would kick her ass if she did. And when he was done, Bo and Luke would take turns kicking her ass, too. But mostly Luke, because Bo'd be too hurt to kick her ass. He'd be too hurt that she would sell herself and dishonor the family like that. And Luke would see how hurt Bo was by it, and that'd make Luke even madder because he can't stand to see Bo hurt. And then they'd have to fight everyone who had the picture? Go out and track every asshole bastard down

132

and punch him, and tear the picture up, or burn it. And Bo, Bo would be burning the very last picture, that they got off this real bad guy who was gonna post it online. And Bo would be about to light it, the very last negative of Daisy, and the bad guy would trip him or something. And Bo would drop the torch and the whole place would catch on fire. And the bad guy would grab the negative and make a break for it. And Luke would be about to follow him, but he looks and sees that Bo's on fire. So Luke grabs a blanket and wraps him in it, before they jump through the flames. And Bo would be coughing, from the smoke, and Luke would say "Are you all right, Cos?" And Bo would say, "Don't worry about me, did he get the negative?" And Luke would say, "Not if we have anything to say about it." And they'd jump in the General just as the bad guy is pulling out. He's desperate to get away with the negative because he's a sick bastard who wants to see Daisy brought down to a whore so he can make money off her. And Bo and Luke realize they could send him heading straight for Mill Creek where the bridge is out. So they put out a fake call on the CB, saying they've decided to run one last shipment of moonshine.

And back in town, Roscoe and Boss Hogg are listening to the CB monitor, and Boss is just about to eat a huge pile of ribs. And he won't share, because he's a Hogg, but Roscoe sneaks a rib from the pile, and just as he's about to take a bite: They hear the Dukes' plan on the CB. And Roscoe runs to the squad, licking his fingers and cursin' them Duke Boys. And he high-tails it to the turn-off just in time to see the porno fucker—who Roscoe thinks is Luke, driving the shine. And the guy sees Roscoe and freaks, and turns down the creek bridge. But before he has time to even think about all the beating off he's gonna do with that picture, he drives through the barricades, airborne, and lands in the creek. His filthy negative is ruined, and Roscoe arrests him for stalking. Because it turns out, Daisy was doing some wash down by the creek, and her clothes got all wet, and she had to take them off for a minute to let them dry in the sun. And while she was waiting that rapist was spying on her with a super powerful lens. And everybody apologizes to Daisy—Uncle Jesse, and Bo, and Luke especially, because he can be a jerk sometimes because he's the oldest, and he was in the Marines. And Luke says he's real sorry he never believed her when she said she didn't know how those pictures happened. Because in his heart he knew that Daisy would not pose for pictures like that because she is pure. And Daisy forgives him, because she knows he was just trying to protect her and Bo both. Because they're kin. They're all each other has in the world. So they have to look out for each other. That is what it means to have a Duke heart.

Excerpt from *A Modern House*

KIRA OBOLENSKY

ELIZABETH, a woman in her thirties to forties. She's building a modern house, in the late 1940s to early 1950s, and a well-known architect has designed it.

ELIZABETH: I went to the site, because it is my house, you know and I had expected that I would be able to walk through it and start to imagine little things like how I might sit by a window to admire the view, and how the kitchen might inspire me to cook a roast, and how the cabinets might open . . . domestic dreams, I suppose, of an apron-wearing hopeless sentimental fool. Because despite the roof falling in, the leaks in the front door, the expense of the excavation, the endless problems with the contractors, I am excited about this house. And I ask one of the men, when the walls are going to go in, you know the goddamn walls in the living room. Excuse me, the GALLERY. And this guy looks at me, he's got actual sympathy in his eyes and he says, "Lady, we got to get the glass special order and it's up in the air." I have all sorts of immediate questions. The first, "up in the air?" The second, a sickening feeling connected to the words "special order." And the third, the final, "glass." Glass? The walls to the house are made of glass? It absolutely defies all human sense, to make a glass house, unless you are trying to teach me some kind of sick lesson. And how we could go through this interminable relationship—oh excuse me, design process, and I would not know Glass, well. How do you expect me to live in a house with no privacy? I am an extremely private person. I'm a doctor. Doctors are not exhibitionists. And here this little baby house sits on its little baby pedestal and you know, it actually looks quite beautiful. A lie, a total and absolute lie. A reception filled with snobs oohing and ahhing about your genius, and not one of them actually has to live in something you designed. Except for me.

Oh, you are an optimist, I can see that, Richard. You think this country survived the first half of the twentieth century, that it's time to reinvent the wheel, it's time to say look at us, we are open, we are free. We are unfettered.

We think that we can dictate what is and is not life. These spaces in the house, they aren't spaces for living, they're places for a display of living. How dare you think we can throw out everything that came before us?

Your wife is quite beautiful. I'd like to meet her.

Excerpt from
Wonderment of Air

DOMINIC ORLANDO

JILL with her boyfriend.

JILL: No, I'm not . . . why do you always get upset when I'm upset? No, I'm not leaving you, I just—we both know I don't have the strength for that—I'm just trying to talk to you.

Something happened in class. Yes, the one you hate. Well, you say it's dumb. I know I already know how to sing, but— why is it so hard to talk to you? The purpose of the class is to bring out—it's a way of offering your voice to, to, okay, fine, The Goddess, or, whatever you want to call it, but it isn't—it's very strong, it's a class about being—The whole idea, the instructor, she—no, no, she's not a—well, maybe she is, but. Like the cathedrals, like Stonehenge, or—to make, with your voice—to make something holy—

Listen to me. They videotaped us—singing, trying to—and at the last class they showed us the videos, and I—there was this one girl. The picture blinked on and she turned, she turned like she was doing something else and just noticed the camera—she turned—*(searching for the word)*—*shyly.* She looked at us shyly and her eyes were so wet and tender and luminous—I never saw anything, anyone, so—and then she started to sing. She opened her mouth very slowly, like she was moving into a kiss, and the sound, the sound that came out of her, I, I, I—I think I started to cry, I think the whole thing, God, Goddess, whatever, it doesn't matter, it isn't, it isn't a word, or an idea or some, some, person—it's a sound, it's a sound, and she, she—

It was me. The girl in the video. I only know because people started coming up to me in the middle of it, just touching me gently on the shoulder, or the arm, just being near me, and the funny thing, the funniest thing—there was nothing familiar about her to me. Nothing at all. She, she was an angel, and me—well, I'm all those things you say, right? I'm a little slow, and, and clumsy, and— what was that great word you used? "Burden." I'm a burden to you. Oh, don't worry, I know. I agree—I woke up next to you this morning and I could feel it, I could feel the burden of being me, just, complete shit—and I dragged myself into the bathroom, and picked up the toothpaste and my brush, and—

And there she was. That girl from the video. With those luminous eyes. And there was the mouth that made that, that incredible sound. And I envied her because I knew no one would call her a burden, no, no, she—she was a prize, a prize, because who wouldn't want an angel in their bed. And if I could, if I was able to think of her as me . . .

But I can't. But somebody will. That's all I wanted to tell you. A prize is something people want to *win*. And I think she'll go. I think if someone comes for her, she'll just—go. And I wanted you to know. That I'm going with her. I just wanted you to know that.

Excerpt from *Falling Flowers*

JEANY PARK

OK YEUN is eighteen years old, and a Korean sexual slave at a Japanese comfort station located in Manchuria in 1944. She is in the infirmary, recovering from a forced abortion and relating the experience to her friend.

OK YEUN: Who would want a baby in this place anyway? Who knows who the father is? I would never want to raise a bastard child. It's not like I had time to get used to the idea, and get attached to her, him—it, whatever.

I never wanted to be a mother. Not me, it was the last thing I ever thought about. *(Silence)*

It's just that I didn't have a say in the matter. *(Beat)*

It's bad enough what they do to me all day long, even when I'm so raw that I'm swollen up like a balloon and I can't stand to have one more man touching me, on top of me, but they keep on coming. One after another, and there's nowhere to go, no escape, not even in my mind. I just want to scream and rip off those ugly, panting faces, like they're getting their revenge, only I don't know what I ever did to them! *(Silence)*

You see, the thing is that when the doctor told me I was pregnant, for a second it all went away and I thought, I could have sworn that I felt something—move inside me. Sort of like a butterfly wing, a quickening. Apparently that's impossible, it was too soon. But I know what I felt. And I couldn't help it. Despite where we are, despite a thousand reasons to hate my life—for that moment, I felt joy. *(Beat)*

And now it's gone.

But why? That's what I can't figure out. Why are they doing this? *(Silence)* They want me to return to work in a week.

Desert Grace

STACEY PARSHALL

A woman enters, thirty-ish, carrying a purse. She sits on a wooden stool.

GRACE: I didn't know which one to kill first. I couldn't decide. I mean, I could have killed either one of them. They both knew it. They had that one moment. You know, that moment when your life flashes before your eyes. They must have. *(Beat)*

Marilyn was my best friend. But Mac, he was my husband. Or should it be, Mac was my husband, but Marilyn was my best friend. You know, neither one of them said they were sorry. *(Beat)*

Our kisses were farther and farther apart. Airy gestures in each other's general direction. But Mac had begun whistling. He'd hum silly little songs under his breath. Stuff that his parents used to listen to, like "Afternoon Delight." I guess I never thought about it. I suppose I should have. It was just nice to hear him whistle.

I finished dressing the baby, who's really a toddler now, but we still call her baby. Our son, Tanner, is seven, and Emma is twelve going on forty. Frightening moments to have your daughter be a bigger grown-up than you are. My excuse was I just didn't have time.

Breakfast was always late, so dishes get rinsed and stacked in our sink. When I get home at six, they're there, crusted and smelling of syrup and old milk. Mac picks Tanner up from his after school program by five, which could get him home by six, before me, but that was "man time."

(Imitates a man's voice) We play ball, we drive around. We just hang out, Mac said when I asked him to start dinner. I would just like to eat earlier than seven. It's too close to the kids' bedtime, I told him. He just kept getting dressed, untying his

socks, turning them from inside out to right side up, but then back again. He could never see the seam across the toe. Then he had this brilliant idea. I know, he says, like he solved world peace. Maybe you should talk with your boss to see if you could switch your hours, start earlier, get off earlier. And you'd do breakfast? I asked. What a joke. Well, he just stood up. He actually stood there, looking down and wiggling his toes, pulling on the pleat of his khakis. He ran his hand down the front of his stomach, turned sideways, and looked in the mirror. Alright, he said, nodding his head.

You'd do breakfast? I asked again. *(Laughs)* I actually stopped for a second. I must have looked half done. My skirt was half zipped, my blouse sticking out of the waistband. And do you know what he asked me? He said, *(Imitates a man's voice)* These pants look good, don't they? He turns around, trying to see his own ass in the mirror. He smiles at himself, like some raging adolescent idiot and leaves. He just walks out of our bedroom.

I watched the back of him, swaying down the hallway in those easy long steps. He passed by Emma's room, not even slowing down. He walked around the laundry basket and over the baby's little push stroller. I heard whistling, him and that song, or maybe it was the sound of the distant yet oncoming train tearing down the tracks straight at me. *(Pause)*

The baby screamed and hollered, and just clutched to my shoulder when I left her at daycare. I sat in the van in the parking lot of Wee World, trying to rub mushed graham cracker wrinkles out of my blouse. And then I remembered. I had a meeting that morning. Henderson and Addle was a huge PR firm that let me know quite often how liberal they were about my parental leave. Six weeks when the baby was born. Kids' check-ups, school stuff. I couldn't walk into the meeting with the mark of motherhood imprinted on my chest. I was told to shine. *(Imitates a man's voice)* You're not the man, like the kids are saying these days? Mr. Henderson, my boss, told me. His skinny body always seemed ready to slide under his desk, which sat around him. Not in front of him, but around him. He looks like a pencil stuck in a pool of mahogany mud. He even has an eraser head, it was flat, with a crew cut. He does seem to be missing a neck to perch it on, though. He goes, "You know that saying 'you the man?' Get it?" He laughed this high-pitched whistle. It drives me nuts. Well, he said, you not the man, you have to look good, he told me. I know. I know, that's pretty shitty. Sexist. But I needed this job, and I needed to make this meeting work. I had to shine. So I quickly turned my van around, racing back to my house. I could have just kept a clean set of clothes at my office, but I was so afraid of making that a living space. I liked home. I had a home.

As I whipped around the corner of our block, I saw Mac's car in the driveway. He probably forgot something, too, I thought. Him being so preoccupied with his nice pants and all. So, I pull in, throw the car in park, cut the engine and run around the side of the house to the kitchen door. I stick the key in the lock, and begin to push. But the curtain of the little window was open a sliver. Just a sliver.

(She jumps, startled by nothing but her own electricity.)

I could see something moving in my kitchen. It was so bizarre. It looked like a huge animal or something. There on my floor. On my no-wax floors. I got this linoleum that is light, kind of off white, like pearls. It has the softest blue design around the edge of each square. It's a sweet blue. Sort of like the sky here. *(Points to the sky)*

That floor is filthy now. *(Begins to cry)*

So, this animal. This . . . beast on my kitchen floor. It's moving around, you know? It's kind of bucking and . . . thrashing. It sorta rolls over a bit, banging up against the cabinet. And then I see through that little sliver, the one from the edge of the curtain, that it has a face. It has two faces.

I must have froze for a second. But then the syrup from this nasty Eggo waffle I choked down while I was feeding our children that morning rose up in my throat. I gagged on it. See, the one face. It was Marilyn. She was on her stomach, or . . . her knees, or something. She looked up, right at the door. She didn't see me, though. Her eyes were closed. Her mouth open. This . . . groan came out of her, her head back. She was totally naked. She's so ugly. *(She wipes snot off her nose with the back of her hand.)*

The other face. Behind her. On her back. Up her ass. Was Mac. My Mac. My precious loving friend-fucking husband, Mac. And he was groaning, too. These deep growls, like some wounded animal.

I knew exactly what to do. It was so clear. First, I didn't throw up, thank you very much. But I didn't go screaming in there, either. O hell no. I've got some dignity, that's for damn sure.

I went back to my car, and called my mother. See, I'm a mom, and I had to think about the kids. Well, she wasn't home. I think on Tuesdays she has some meeting or something. This women's thing for some charity, I'm sure. But I left her a message and told her to pick up the kids for me.

Then I get back out of the car, and go to our garage. I even walked past that window, but didn't look in. I didn't have to. I will remember. I will always have burned into my mind that picture of the two of them, on my floor . . . my clean no-wax floor. Fuck. My kids play on that floor.

So, in the garage, on the top shelf above the workbench, we have this red locked box. I take it down, and unlock the combination. I remembered the combination. See, I'm so smart. I really am. I mean, shit. I work, and I'm great at my job. And I take care of the house, and my three kids. I pay all the bills. I take care of the insurance. Hell, I even take care of our 401(k)s and our stock options. I do that, because I'm the smart one. ME! I'M THE SMART ONE! I know they didn't think so. I'm sure they thought I was so stupid I wouldn't figure out what was going on. But I would have found out. For sure I would have known. He never hummed songs about me anymore. He hasn't since we were in college, when we fell in love. I think it was love. I don't know. I don't know shit. *(Beat)* He never made those noises with me.

I went to the front door, which was also unlocked. Fuckin' idiot. I crept through the entryway, down the hallway to the kitchen in the back. I slipped my shoes off, so they didn't even hear me. But I had to make them stop. I just had to. I walked right up behind them, behind Mac and aimed the gun at him. He still didn't hear me standing there. He didn't even FEEL me standing there. Now, I would think that if you're going to die, something inside of you should click. Something in your brain, or in your gut would tell you to freeze. To stop. To look up. To get the fuck off the whore! But not Mac, he's so stupid! He deserves—

(Pause. She sits and stares, like she's first noticing something out the window.)

It was . . . It just popped. I could feel the bullet slide smoothly, and precisely out the gun.

Well, he screams! Like a little girl. It was high and loud! And Marilyn, that bitch! She's screaming too. I know the bullet didn't go through Mac and hurt her 'cuz she pushes him off of her, or he gets off her. I'm not sure. It's all kind of a blur! There was blood on my floors, and they're screaming, and crying. Fuckin' Mac, he's like O my God! O my God! Let's hope God can help him, now. Motherfucker.

And Marilyn—she wouldn't quit screaming, so I just shot her, too. She was just laying there, naked, her ugly white fleshy body next to my husband.

(She pauses, then looks around.)

You got anything stronger? *(Giggles)*

Than coffee?

No. You don't? Uhmmm . . . a lunch special then? The homemade corn tortilla, eggs, black beans, chilies and this killer salsa thing it says right here. It's pretty good? *(Pause)*

What mountain is that? The Sangre de Crisco. Do people around here think the mountains can talk to you? Or do they just listen?

(She opens her purse, digs through her wallet, takes out a picture. She stares at it, and then holds it up as if to show somebody.)

That's my husband. He's dead, now. He was a tragedy.

Excerpt from
Red Light, Green Light

ERIK PATTERSON

RUTH: I've read up.
Believe me, I've done my research.
I've read the books.
I've read the magazines.
I've rented the films.
I've watched the news programs.
I've even searched the web.
I've culled my data.
You know, the thing that's . . . *difficult* . . . about being a parent,
is that you never know what your kid knows,
what your kid's not telling you,
what your kid's doing when you're not there.
So you have to fill in the blanks,
connect the dots.
And while I might not know what you,
my son,
specifically have done,
I do know what people say—
about you,
about you people,
your people,
about you and your people.
I know what you do, as a group.
I know about, about, about—
I know all about the anonymous sex.

I know about
sex with strangers,
in clubs—sex clubs—with towels around your waists.
About sex in places like public parks behind trees,
or urinals, public restrooms like George Michael,
or alleys, dark alleys, orgies in alleys,
multiple partners in one night, countless strangers.
I know about glory holes,
which I have to admit have a kind of spectacular name:
Glory Hole.
It paints a vivid picture:
Glory Hole.
I found this website that lists all of the glory holes in the world,
at least that's what the website purports,
and I'm inclined to believe it
because there are just so many bathrooms listed, it's . . .
dizzying.
And the website has all of this . . . *data*, I guess you'd call it.
About where to find the best glory holes in your area, and what
time to go, you know . . . when each hole hits heavy
traffic. If you wanted to get your penis sucked by a stranger dur-
ing your lunch hour, believe me, I could point you in the right
direction.
I know about,
about,
about—
I know about leather bars, about bear bars.
About size queens, muscle queens, queen queens.
About cock rings.
Anal beads.
Lube.
Poppers.
I know there are other drugs, but poppers are so scary because
they could damage your brain, just like that, so you have to be
real careful.
And overdosing on Viagra, and things like that.

146

Because, you know,
the gay population is using a lot of Viagra these days.
And I know about, um,
um,
tops and bottoms, also known as "pitchers" and "catchers,"
and then there are versatile guys but I haven't read of a baseball
term that describes them.
I was thinking "he plays for both teams" might work
but then I found out that already means something else entirely.
And I know about, um,
two-headed dildos,
and things like that.
I don't really want to get into all of the sex toys
because they're kind of disgusting to me—
I can't even figure out what some of them are even used for,
I just know that they're disgusting.
        (Beat)
But what I'm trying to say is that there are all of
these,
these,
these images in my head.
And you have to understand that these
images
sometimes make you a very difficult person to talk to.
But that's not all.
Because I know it's not just difficult for me.
I'm not that self-absorbed.
I'm not that—
I know how you . . .
I know, I know—
I mean, I don't *know*, but I can imagine,
how difficult it must have been for you,
must *be* for you,
to—
oh, God, to, to—
To come out.

To have that conversation.
To keep having that conversation.
To keep having to have that—
It must have been so hard.
When you said it the first time.
The fear of rejection.
The fear of other things.
The fear of—
I tried not to reject you when you told me.
Because I suspected.
Your son reaches his twenties without ever bringing a girl home
and you start to suspect.
And I saw the way you looked at your, you know,
male friends
and the way you weren't looking at your, you know,
female friends.
So I prepared myself,
just in case,
so as not to have the reaction I didn't want to have, which was
one of rejecting you.
But, Caleb, honey . . .
You have to understand
that if *I'm* having these thoughts—
I, your mother—
if these thoughts are in *my* head,
then just think about what other people must be thinking.
I can't help it.
And what I've read,
what I've seen—
which hasn't all been bad.
I don't want to give you that impression . . .
     (Beat)
But people are backwards,
people don't understand,
people have a long way to go, you know?
And when they see you,

148

what some of them are thinking,
what I know some of them are thinking—
I mean, when they see you, I know they're not: Seeing. You.
They're seeing—
They're—

(Beat. She's begun to run out of steam.)
And I know about Matt Shepard.
Everyone calls him Matthew, but I read somewhere that his friends called him Matt.
I know what happened to him.
And my first thought is that plenty of straight people die worse deaths than he did without getting put on a pedestal. Without getting idealized. Without becoming heroes.
But I understand why he haunts us.
Because it's just terrible what they did to him.
And you could say it was just a moment of passion,
but that defense doesn't stick because they just spent too much time with him.
They lured him into their truck.
And then they started beating him.
And then they continued to beat him as they drove him out to the fence.
The fence where they were going to leave him.
I know all about Matt Shepard.
And things like what happened to him—they could happen to the rest of us too,
but when you factor in a thing like sexuality,
the chances of something like that happening to my son,
they triple, or something terrible like that.
And that scares me, Caleb. It really, really scares me.
(Beat)
And I know about AIDS.
And I know you don't want me to say it,
but I'm a mother,
so I'm going to say it:
You need to be wearing a condom,

and your partner needs to be wearing a condom—
because things were better for awhile,
but lately people have become lackadaisical,
and the figures are rising.
So just wear a condom.
Just do it.
For me.
Because the thought of you getting AIDS
scares the shit out of me.
I'm sorry.
I'm sorry that I'm like this.
I don't mean to sound like a Public Service Announcement.
But I'm a mother,
I'm your mother,
and I just—
I don't want you to get hurt.
That's all.
     (Beat)
That's all.
So.
What are you having for lunch?

Phyllis

MARY JO PEHL

Last night I called my bank, the automated phone service—the number you can call to find out information about your account. You know, that lady who answers will give you that information but only if you have a touchtone phone and you enter the number of the desired service followed by the pound sign. The lady who used to give me that information was "Phyllis." Most people don't know that's her name, that she even has a name but she does—it's Phyllis. Everyone's probably talked to Phyllis at one time or another—she's the gal who gives you the actual telephone number when you dial directory assistance; or she directs your call for most people's voice mail; or she'll tell you, "The number is no longer in service."

Phyllis and I talk a lot. It seems that no matter when I call, Phyllis is always on duty. And she thanks me for calling but she never ever acknowledges that we've spoken dozens of times before. I guess I thought we were starting to get to know each other, even just a little bit. After all, she's the only person in the whole wide world who knows my secret code. I wondered if working for the bank in such a prestigious position wasn't making her a little bit haughty—maybe she thought she was too good to say "Hey! How are you doing?" every now and then. Still, I want to trust her. Even if she did sound kind of judgmental when I inquired about my checking account balance. She never really said anything—it was just the way she said, "Your checking account balance is four dollars and seventy-three cents." It was kind of uncomfortable and I tried to explain my situation to her but it just seemed like . . . I remember once

I tried to transfer funds from checking to savings so I pressed three and when I entered the dollar amount, Phyllis paused and told me there were insufficient funds to make that transaction. There was an awkward silence . . . and—and I think we both knew that it wasn't anybody's fault . . . Then she just hung up. I think she was as embarrassed as I was. It's not like I'm mad at her or anything. I guess we got along okay. We had a cordial working relationship. A couple of times I asked her if she wanted to get together after work, maybe meet me for happy hour somewhere, but she always acted like she didn't hear me. She would just say something like "Possible error. Please press the star sign for the main menu." And she was stubborn—she refused to acknowledge that I didn't want the main menu. There was some sort of wall around Phyllis. You could only get so close. I tried not to take it personally—I bet that someone, somewhere probably hurt Phyllis very, very badly and she probably wouldn't trust anyone for a long, long time. Then I called Phyllis last night, just to talk and ask her if check number 19,584 had cleared but a different voice answered the phone. There was a new gal manning the phones. This new gal sounded kind of flighty, rather immature. I don't know her name—she sounded like a Kelly or—or a Lori, probably. Sure, Lori seemed nice but maybe just a little too nice, like she was setting me up to stab me in the back. Like I'd ask her to transfer some money from savings to checking and she'd say sure, then take all the money and go to Mexico and you'd never see her again. Or I'd ask her about my savings account balance and she'd say "What savings account, bitch?!" and laugh madly. I think the worst part is that nobody—nobody—has said word one about Phyllis—it's like Phyllis never existed. I tried to ask Lori. I brought up Phyllis's name real casual but Lori pretended like I didn't say anything. Then I tell myself, well, I shouldn't pry . . . maybe it's none of my business . . . Then I think . . . maybe I don't want to know. Maybe the bank has some sort of police state, oppressive, regime-like corporate structure like Pinochet's Chile or Romania when Ceausescu was in power, and one day Phyllis just disappears and everything with her. Her files are gone, her family photos, and the picture of her dog—gone—and the email that she saved about the Dalai Lama's advice for life that she printed out and hung in her cube—gone. Suddenly there's Lori and nobody says nothing, nobody knows nothing, and nobody asks nothing. Maybe Gary at the weather number knows something.

Excerpt from *Barrio Hollywood*

ELAINE ROMERO

AMA enters handcuffed. She is forty-eight years old. Her son, Alex, a boxer, was injured during a boxing match and wasn't expected to recover. Ama has been arrested for the mercy killing.

AMA: My son. My child is dead. And you blame me? He killed him. Michael took Alex's throat in his hands and he killed him. I saw the whole thing. That horrible man murdered my son. I *am* a witness! I want that man to go to the electric chair! I want him dead! Let him feel what it feels like to be murdered. *(More upset)* My son was going to be fine. He had a difficult few months, but he was going to be fine. *(Short beat)* I did not sneak off. I went out for some air. *(Short beat)* No, I did not know he was dead when I left. I had no idea until you said it to me. What do you mean—contradicting myself? *(Beat)* You already have ideas in your head. I can see them floating around in there. I can see that! I didn't go to school. I don't have perfect English like you, but I can see this. This is not right. I saw everything. Don't pretend. When you know. *(Breaking down)* The truth.

Let me see Graciela. She knows why this happened. *(To herself)* Taking me from my church. From my prayers. When my God comforts me. That's who I love. That's who I listen to. *El siempre está conmigo.* You and your fancy cars. You and your guns. You've never done nothing good for me. *(Short beat; yelling to someone as if he's leaving)* Give me back my suitcase! My son gave me that. *Para mi cumpleaños.* For my birthday trip. He's giving it to me as a gift. When Graciela turns thirty, I turn forty-eight. Only two days apart. *(Getting emotional)* I saw that pretty island on Channel 52. I saw it in *Spanich.* It was a beautiful place with canaries up in the trees. And water—bluer than

154

your eyes. You can see little canaries there like lizards in the desert. Singing all the time. Making everybody happy. And everybody could be happy if some people let God do His job.
(Ama starts crying.)

Simple things. That's all I ever wanted. *(Short beat)* I didn't kill Alex with my hands but by wanting so much. And he wanted so much to give me those things. He fought when he was bleeding. When he couldn't see. He fought for money. But I kept wanting more. And you know how God feels about that! You must accept what He gives you. And smile. BECAUSE THAT IS HOW GOD WORKS! He makes the rules. He decides. And you take it. Whatever hand you're dealt. But you gotta keep your poker face on. You gotta look like you're winning or you lose that much more. My grandfather taught me that. He was a poker player from Chihuahua. He knew how to fool people into believing him. *(Quickly)* That's not what I meant.

Excerpt from
An Unfinished Room

MARK ROSENWINKEL

NAOMI is a young activist nun preparing herself for an act of civil disobedience at an animal research site. She speaks to a reluctant middle-aged professor.

NAOMI: You're damn right you're angry. An angry young man. Well, maybe not young, but . . . There's nothing to be afraid of. You can't live in this world without getting angry at something. In fact, you're probably more angry than the rest of us. Because you bury it so deep. Look at me. Yes, yes. I can see it. Underneath a thin veneer of inhibition and shyness, there's fire, and passion. Oh, yes, I can see it. You're so full of passion, it scares you and you hide it. But don't worry, you're in good company. Why do you think I'm doing this? I could have gone off, gotten some nice secretarial job. Maybe ended up running some company. What would that prove? People I went to school with, they're all running around in cars and boats, big houses in the suburbs. And here I sit, hunkered down in the dirt, ready to put myself in jail. And why? Because I have passion! And so do you, or you wouldn't be here. Don't be ashamed. Revel in it! I mean, who do you think Christ was anyway, some anemic white guy on sympathy cards? He was a firebrand, a rebel, a man of ultimate passion. The saints, they speak of being ravished by Him. Do you hear me? Do you follow me, Cab? They imagined themselves actually being taken up by this, this power, this driving, divinely passionate force . . .

(Suddenly realizing she's getting carried away)

I'm sorry. I don't know why I said that. I have to confess, I've been thinking of leaving the church. It's getting harder for

156

me to remain an obedient member of the flock when I feel so strongly about these things. You understand me, don't you? There's all kinds of . . . crap that's going on in the world, and I've got to do something about it. It's like a craving, an insatiable drive . . . "The thing I don't want to do, that I do." And the thing that I do want, that I don't do. Here they come. Lie down! If they give you any trouble, kick them right where it counts. We shall be the thorn in their flesh, the obstacle in their side! Sssssh! Come on now! No turning back! NO TURNING BACK! . . .

    (Sings)
    "We shall, we shall, we shall not be moved . . . "

Excerpt from
Tearing Down the Walls

ELLENA ANTOINETTE (TINA) SCHOOP

Sitting in front of a brownstone building, a woman in her sixties is talking to her granddaughter. The woman, GRANDMA, is clutching a piece of paper in her hand.

GRANDMA: Ms. Mary Mack, Mack, Mack,
  All dressed in black, black, black
  With silver buttons, buttons, buttons. All down her back, back, back.
  Sssshhhhhhhhh. Hear it?
  Sssshhhhhh, this street, this street, used to be filled with so many young dreamers, clappin', double Dutch, laughing . . . hear it?
  Gwen, run!!
  The building on the corner—that one. Andre, Joe, and Mackenzy, made them a little trampoline. They wanted to make it to the Olympics—Joe, he could fold his body in ways make me believe he had no bones.
  Anyway, Ms. Mary Mack, all dressed in black,
  Them silver buttons. Where's Gwen?
  Legend has it, she was always dressed in black. Mary, Mary Mackenzy. You could still maybe catch a glimpse of her parading down the boulevard. Yes, parading.
  Mary Mackenzy. See, she was the illegitimate child of Adam and Eva Mae. Adam Whitfield and Eva Mae Jordan that is. But they was church-going folks and didn't want nobody to know Eva Mae was out there . . . doing . . . you know? She went away.

Eva Mae. Child ain't you listening? They sent her away to have her baby. They never saw her after that. So . . . Ms. Mary Mack—Mary Mackenzy, born to Adam and Eva Mae—still walking the boulevard—looking . . . for love maybe? in them dark corners . . . Building empty now, where's Gwen? Where is everybody?

Joe, I think he won the silver. That damn Andre, got himself strung out. Nothing left on this block but me, a bunch of old boarded up flats and . . . every once in a while . . . Mary's shadow. C'mon child, now, we gotta go . . . Gwen not dead. Who said Gwen dead. Hush child.

(Boulders and bulldozers start barreling down the street—dust flying, silver buttons dropping.)

Excerpt from *Thrown by Angels*

GWENDOLYN SCHWINKE

BABY is fifteen. She speaks to her sister, Sissy, who is seventeen. Their father has kept them locked in a basement for seven years, telling them the world has come to an end. Baby has escaped, and now has returned for her sister.

BABY: Sissy, two nights ago when I ran off, I was so scared. You know I haven't been out of this basement since we came here seven years ago. But I couldn't help myself. That night I looked over at him and I could not stand it, I could not stand to be next to him, I could not stand to be in this house any more. The window was open there in his room. Just the screen was on it, and outside . . . I could see outside. Upstairs there he has windows and some wind was coming in and I could see some trees. He went to sleep, and I just looked out that window, and smelled, and listened. Something was out there. So I stood up on the bed, and I took a couple big bounces, and I jumped right at that screen. It crashed away, and I was out! I was on the ground, and I just ran as fast as I could into the woods. Out there the trees are thick, and I'm littler than him, I'm faster, he couldn't catch me and I just kept running. He kept screaming that I wouldn't make it, that the world was ended and I wouldn't last, but this thought happened to me, Sissy, this thought . . . this thought just popped into my head like something you'd see in those little bubbles in the funny papers. Remember that? Remember the funny papers? Where people talk in bubbles? I don't know why I remembered the bubbles, but I did, and this is the thing that was in my bubble: Fuck You! And then I said it out loud: Fuck You. And I realized that it was a prayer. It's not a prayer you kneel for—it's a prayer you pray when you're running. So for hours and hours I ran, and I prayed: Fuck You.

Excerpt from *Thrown by Angels*

GWENDOLYN SCHWINKE

The biblical figure of LOT'S WIFE *gives her version of what really happened at the burning of Sodom and Gomorrah.*

LOT'S WIFE: The night before, before the fire, two angels came to our house to spend the night. And a bunch of men who lived in the town came all around our house. They knew the angels were there, somehow they knew something bad was going to happen and they wanted them to come out, or they were going to break down the door. But the angels wouldn't go out.

They are pounding on the door, and pounding on all the windows. Some of their faces are smashed against the windows, people I know, my friends, angry, smashed against the windows of my house. They want to break it down, break it open, pull out the angels, like the meat of a nut. They want them. Must have them, someone, or they will destroy us all. They are taunting us, these angry faces I know at my windows. Dirty, they say, you call us dirty? Clean us up, then, you angels. We'd like something really clean.

To stop them, then, my husband, Lot, he takes our daughters and shoves them out the door. He says, "Take these girls. They're clean. Leave the angels alone and take my daughters." I try to reach them, but he shuts the door. I pull it open. He pushes. I pull. Push, pull, push, pull, finally I get my head and shoulders out and he shuts me in the door. I can't move, but this is what I see:

My daughters, my two little girls, are thrown into a crowd of angry men. The men are yelling, pushing. At first it looks like the girls will be crushed. Then one man grabs the oldest girl and lifts her up. Another man grabs her, too, and they hold her up. Over the crowd, for the men to see. And then the younger. Up, up, all these hands holding them, their dresses all messed up. The girls are crying, screaming. But the men get very quiet. Then one man who is holding the youngest, pulls her down, in an embrace. The older, too, someone holds her tight, then sets her down. They hug the girls and set them gently on the front step. Someone brushes away their tears. Straightens their dresses. They stumble away, these men. They are crying, crying so hard they cannot see.

Excerpt from *Sirius Rising*

GWENDOLYN SCHWINKE

ALBERTA, a farm woman in the middle of life, speaks to the audience.

ALBERTA: I'll tell you what it takes: devotion. Pure devotion. You devote yourself to a farm. It's just like a marriage. It takes work to make things hold together, make sure they don't plumb fall apart, bust into pieces and scatter to the winds. I know, I was married for thirty years and we didn't stay together by love alone. Work had a lot to do with it.

We stacked bales in that hay barn, standing up under the rafters in hundred-and-ten degree heat. We chopped ice on that pond at fifteen below just so the cows could get something to drink. And when I think of all the miles we walked over this farm looking for lost calves, rounding up cows, if we could have strung those miles together, we probably would have ended up halfway around the world. But it's a good thing we didn't do that, because then we would have had to walk home.

I tell you, all that work, and nothing was as hard as the work I did to keep my marriage all of a piece. I'll tell you a secret, sometimes I couldn't tell what I was working on, my farm or my marriage. When your husband is gone on a hunting trip and he was supposed to fix the fence before he went, and the cows get out and there you are at midnight running down the county road, trying to round up sixteen Herefords before they all get hit by cars, tell me, what is it that you are working on?

When you go off to town for a shopping trip and you forget to turn off the water tank so that when you come home your calves are belly-deep in sludge because you flooded the holding pen, and there's your husband knee-deep beside them. And you see the look in his eyes. And when you pick up a shovel right then and there before you even go to change your clothes, tell me, what are you trying to save? Those calves or your marriage? Your marriage or the farm? 'Cause in the end, I realized they were the same to me.

But, gosh darn it, Elmer, you had to go and die anyway. I worked so hard, and you still left me behind. Sometimes I think I'm not going to get to join you until I've worked hard enough. So I stay here and I keep on working. My kids think I'm too old to do it, they think I'm going to hurt myself. "Go on, Mom," they say, "Why do you stay on that old place? Why don't you move to town?" "Why don't I move to town?" Because this is my life here, Elmer's and mine, and I ain't running out on our marriage just because he's dead.

Excerpt from *Stone Lilies*

BUFFY SEDLACHEK

MOLLY *(age seventeen):* I miss my brothers. Strappin' big boyos. They was so good to me. I dunno why they can't come and fetch me. Why don't they know where to look? Aw, we'd have such laughs on each other alla time, and they taught me all the important things a girl should know ta stay outa trouble, 'cause lord knows, m' Da, He's embarrassed of all of it. But, the boyos—especially Michael. They was always remindin' me about the time a the month that might be comin', and the parts of a boy that should never touch any parts of a girl, and funny stories about girls getting pregger when they ain't ever even seen a boy's parts or had their panties down around their knees, how about that? Oh, m' Da woulda thunk they was being sinful and dirty-mouth, but they took it as their sacred duty to protect me from the wicked ways of the world. I miss 'em sometimes, something awful. There's nothing here they coulda imagined they needed to tell me. But, if anybody ever comes for me, if I get outa here, I'll be telling 'em all of it, every breath and every smell and sound and sight. Burnt into my brain like a brand. They don't know. Or they'd come for me. I'm sure the priest convinced Da it was for my own good to leave our village. Too pretty, he says. Moral danger. Especially without me mam.

(She spits.)

Moral danger. He's the one in danger. He put his hands on me. I bit him. I bit a man of god. Right on the wrist. He tasted just the same as anybody else, too.

Chinese Rug

AMY SEHAM

One day this very famous playwright, I'm sure you would have heard of him—he's won the Pulitzer prize, and at least one Tony, I think. Well, he was in town at the professional theatre down the street from my little theatre. It's funny, they're only about three blocks apart—three blocks and several million dollars. Well he knew someone who worked for us, I guess. I'm not sure why he came in, but I got to talking to him—and it was incredible. I showed him a monologue I was working on and he read it through and he talked with me about it. Terrific stuff—good criticism. He really understood. I could see why he was so—great—so successful. But more than that. We went for a drink and he was telling me about the play he was writing now. I felt honored—like I was the first one to hear about it—two playwrights discussing their work—when he reached over and pinched my breast. Well—I was so—I don't know—I didn't know what to do, so I kind of ignored it. Don't be uptight, I said to myself. What's really wrong with that? It's free and sensual and kind of sixties or something. Why not—really? Then he suggested that we go to my place because, he said—he wanted to wash my beautiful hair. Of course I knew that it wasn't about washing my hair—but I wanted—I didn't want to lose him—lose his interest—in me—in my work—in me. I flirted around it for a while. Why are these things so difficult for me? But finally I said coyly—it's disgusting to remember the little girl voice—We'll need to buy some shampoo—I don't have any at home. So we did. We bought a bottle of Johnson's baby shampoo and we went to my apartment. I pretended we were really going to wash my hair. Why not? It was just the kind of poetic thing that artists do together. But part of me was in horror of him seeing me naked in the bright light of the bathroom. My breasts would sag—my stomach would roll, my hair would be wet. Better to lie on my back in the dark. So in the end, when we never went to the bathtub at all, I told myself it was just as well. We were on the floor. He was big—powerful—eager. I was—I'm just not good at this stuff—I was completely passive. I knew he was getting impatient. I knew I was disappointing him. He pulled my head down to his cock. I took it in my mouth. Then, I just started crying. There on my knees on the blue and white Chinese rug my parents gave me for my thirtieth birthday with his cock in my mouth and tears running down my cheeks—I felt like a fool. He pulled away and looked at me. "I know," he said. "It ruins everything, doesn't it?"

My god! He understands! He understands that it does, somehow, ruin everything. I nodded, staring at the floor. "I don't know why," I whispered—kind of choked, you know.

Then he said, "You have an idea of a meeting of souls, but that's not what it turns out to be." I looked up at him. He was looking at me—but I mean right into my eyes. He said, "And then, instead, it's humiliating and kind of animal." I was—in awe—I guess. How did he know what was going on inside me? "I know," he said. "I know." And then he reached around my head and pulled me back down.

Holy War

ROSANNA STAFFA

Every morning I wake up and reach, then I remember: I don't smoke. I gave up. It's been years and years. First time I smoked a cigarette it was with Piera, waiting for bus 94 across from Bar Magenta. After that cigarette there was another, and another. I smoked because it was something I could do and do it well. Mornings I wished I hadn't gotten out of bed, well the cigarette was there on the kitchen table, waiting like an old dog. Days I wished I hadn't been born, or I had been born a chimp, a man, a psychopath killer or anything at all but me, before I knew it a Marlboro was between my lips, easy as that, smooth as silk. On weekends Piera and I played cards and smoked. Or just smoked. We felt quite mysterious, sending little puffs in the air. Matches came in tiny square boxes, thin stubby rolls of paper and wax. With practice you could open the roll and form a little cone, and when you lit the top a ballerina twirled in the air, burning. I was a bit of a worry to Piera. I didn't send matches flying in the air, didn't land a job, didn't drive, and was allergic to this and that. To hear Piera, I got an itch and a rash just by looking at the big blue sky. "The bastards are killing us," Piera said. I didn't know who the bastards were, but I had an inkling one was Signor Rosini, her boss. I felt a bit squeamish about Signor Rosini who wore suspenders and yelled bloody this and bloody that. Secretly I felt there was something in being martyred by a man who spit big wads of tobacco in large spittoons. But it wasn't only Signor Rosini who was out to get us. Piera hinted at corporations tainting the food, the water even. It was a holy fucking war. Well one night that Piera was lighting matches and sending them flying in the air, she gave me a long look. "Hey, cigarettes could kill us you know," and in that moment, me and her sitting in my kitchen, with matches going up like fireflies, I saw everybody looking for us, and they couldn't find us. We were gone. We were dead. I saw them run up and down elevators and buses. Frantic. I saw them sticking their heads here and there, looking for us. Calling, calling. Well they didn't. It turned out that nobody looked but me when Piera died. She got sick and died, like that. She wanted to go fast when her time came, and she sure made it the fastest journey, the bullet train from Tokyo to wherever. She took no luggage. She said no goodbyes. Her sister lived out of town and took Piera home, like that. Her sister didn't call me about a memorial service or anything. I didn't know if there was one. So I did my own thing. For a few days I kept calling the office: "Is Piera there?" I'd ask. I called from this phone booth and an old lady answered "No," each time. One night I sat at the kitchen table, opened a pack of Marlboros and smoked every cigarette, one after the other. I could smell the first time Piera and I smoked together and every time after that. One after the other. When I was done, I was done forever. Really done. I haven't smoked a cigarette ever since. No cigarettes for me. When I used to smoke I carried my day home with me, in the smell in my sweater. I took home every moment, like a thief. I go home clean now. I take home nothing.

Excerpt from *Lenin's Shoe*

SAVIANA STANESCU

JASNA is Serbian-Romanian, a former war-correspondent in Sarajevo, now in New York. Kebab is a homeless Muslim, failed suicide bomber, now in his own world.

Lights up on the street.

Jasna feeds Kebab with soup. He's like a baby, waiting for her to put the spoon in his mouth.

JASNA: There you are . . . I knew we'd get along. I don't care who you are. You're Kebab. My Kebab. You speak the most beautiful language: Silence . . . You don't play smart . . . You're scared . . . It's all right to be scared . . . It's all right . . .

You're a good boy . . . You don't ask me why I stopped being a journalist. That's good . . . That's why I'll probably tell you. Not right now. Maybe later . . . Let's talk about you now. I can read in your eyes: war and failure . . .

And the funny thing is: I'm happy to see a sad face like yours. I know, it's not very nice to say that, but you don't understand English, so I'm half excused. I miss sad faces, isn't that awful? Here, in America, you read "success" in people's eyes, they all throw at you that perfect smile, those perfect teeth I'll never be able to have . . . Do you like this chicken noodles soup? Yes, you like it . . . Plus, they have such clear goals. They go to war and kill for something precise, for oil, for college money, for career, for a swimming pool, for a family vacation in the Caribbean, for wearing Armani, for having fun, for being happy, for being a hero, a star, number one . . . *(Kebab spits the chicken out.)* Why did you spit out the meat, it's not pork! . . . Okay, no meat, only the noodles . . .

What do *we* fight and kill for? For being unhappy. For saving our unhappiness. We fight for the right of suffering in our own languages. Isn't that silly? . . . Is it silly? To die for a language . . . Why shall I die for a word? . . .

You should learn English, it's a powerful language . . . It helps you set precise goals for yourself. And once you have a clear goal for tomorrow, life becomes easier. I grew to like short-term goals. My immediate one is related to you. *(She takes out of her bag a pair of shoes.)* Tah-dah-dam! New old shoes for you! Jasna's husband's. Another Big Foot loser . . .

Did I tell you that I couldn't sleep with him after I got back home from Sarajevo? I couldn't sleep with anyone. The last man I slept with was that Spanish guy from Barcelona, a photographer for Associated Press. Pedro. He wanted to go home, but he stayed with me. I was scared. Even the BBC guys had left Sarajevo that morning . . . We made love the whole night. Some night! Bombs and orgasms . . . Big deaths, little deaths . . . Next evening, I and Pedro got drunk with some Bosnian soldiers. Waiting for the night bombings. The soldiers, crazy guys, stripped their uniforms and drew targets on their bare chests . . . I remember so well that day . . . We were having so much fun . . .

But you can never hear those mortar bombs coming. You only hear the bullets and tell yourself: they were not for me! . . . You get used to that . . . You can even drink calmly your beer. Like Pedro. Before saying "Fuck. I've been hit!" . . . *(Beat)* His coffin was my ticket out of Sarajevo. I thought I should buy him a suit to be buried in, but I decided a white T-shirt was okay. It was only later when I realized that I bought poor Pedro an American T-shirt . . . *(Beat)* Well . . . Kebab . . . When you start telling intimate things to complete strangers, it's high time to close your business and write your memories, isn't it? Or maybe it's high time to start living. *(She looks around, makes sure no one can see her, and kisses Kebab.)*

171

Excerpt from *Waxing West*

SAVIANA STANESCU

DANIELLA, thirty-one, Romanian, she came to New York as a mail-order bride; Charlie, forty-one, American, computer freak. Charlie is immersed in his work on a laptop.

DANIELLA: It's only vitamin C, Charlie. Orange flavored, with rose hips. 6.89 dollars . . . 6.89 dollars are capable to drive you mad at me, Charlie. That's how much your "love" is worth in your opinion. Not seven dollars, not seventy, not seven hundred . . . No, you love me for exactly six dollars and eighty-nine cents. My hips are worth less than some chewable anonymous tablets with rose hips . . . *(Beat)* Okay Charlie. It's your choice. I don't want to remind you what I do for you for free. I don't smoke here. I cook for you. Romanian food! . . . I hate Romanian food, Charlie, I hate *sarmale* and *mamaliga* and the Romanian traditional smell, and the Romanian exotic flavors, and the Romanian claustrophobic kitchens, but for you Charlie, I stick two cotton pads in my nostrils, I play my energizing tape with applauses, and I do it for you Charlie, I cook for you, although I hate this verb *cook* and I plan to make it disappear in all languages. *(Beat)* And it's not only about cooking, Charlie, although everything is about cooking. I play with you, that silly Thanksgiving game you love, every Sunday at 6 P.M., you get all naked except for your white silly socks, and you take the "turkey" position, and I have to pretend that I put you in the oven, and that the fire goes stronger and stronger, and I have to see your silly dick reacting to that, Charlie, instead of my body, I have to act as if I cook you, Charlie because you're a turkey, and I have to show you a plastic knife and say "Oh, I'm gonna eat you turkey," and I play this silly part, Charlie, and see you coming and shouting of pleasure when I start cutting you with the plastic knife, and I have to say "Oh, you're such a good turkey, yum-yum," but I don't yum-yum, and I don't like to yum-yum, and I don't generally eat meat, so I yum-yum only for your sake . . .

And now you're mad at me because I *stole* this damn plastic jar: Orange flavored chewable vitamin C-500 . . . I just took it from the shelf and put it in my bag. The Calvin Klein bag you gave me for Christmas. Nobody saw me, so what's your problem, Charlie? And you know what: the bag from you is not a real Calvin Klein!

Excerpt from *Honeymoon*

DANE STAUFFER

NORMA is a middle-aged housewife starting out on her own after years of a barely fulfilling marriage.

NORMA *(Selling water purifiers door to door):* This health guard sentinel will clean up any impurities that you and your family may . . . I'm sorry, I'm just gonna dispense with my script here Mr. *(Looking)* Zydecker. Let's face it, water's bad and it's going to kill us if we don't all buy these here sentinels. It may be too late to clean it up at the source, but why should you suffer? I'm not just trying to make a fast buck, Mr. Z, I believe in this product! I'm not just some housewife out trying to earn a nest egg so she can leave her husband who behaves as if we perpetually live in the 1950s. I am not trying desperately to establish my own identity so I can overcome my fears that my life has been wasted on ungrateful children who rejected the plot of lawn we worked so hard to give them. I am not afraid my life has been insufficient, I am not trying to assert my rights as a woman, I am just trying— to make—a—sale! Can I come in? Thank you!!

Excerpt from
Magnificent Waste

CARIDAD SVICH

LIZZIE takes another hit of oxygen as her face comes up on TV screen. A vérité moment caught by the camera.

LIZZIE B: So, I go into this bar to get oxygen, 'cause that's what you do now. You put on a mask. You breathe pure fucking air. You feel exhilarated and alive. The bar is dark and the lights are blue and the attitude is like something out of *Naked Lunch* and the music is at minimum 'cause that's what the place is about, getting to the minimal thing in life: Air, breath, oxygen, right?

And after you've been tranced-out raved up pumped down blissed out broken by every beat and kicked in the solar like an avalanche, oxygen feels good, it feels right, 'cause you've had every smart drug you can imagine, and they didn't make you any smarter, and the stupid ones are old stand-bys, and heroin and cocaine are too damn rock star tragic to seduce anymore, and E, well, it doesn't last, does it? Ecstasy is a dream, and Prozac is a letdown, and placebos do no good, and absinthe is the only thing really worth craving for, except you have to hunt for it, don't you? Underground, in New Orleans, San Francisco, at the low end of the meat district in New York, and that gets fucking tiring, 'cause wormwood isn't potent, not like in the Shelley and Byron days, and you want to believe the hallucinogens are working, but it takes too damn long, and there's no time anymore, not to waste, so oxygen is what you end up with. It makes you feel human again, 'cause it reminds you, right? It reminds you of being a person, of what you're made of. Pure fucking air.

I used to believe in art, but that got as boring as drugs and it didn't get me anywhere, not fast enough, so I changed my view. I put on a pair of mirrored sunglasses and started to reflect everything around me. I started picking up kids off the street. Hungry kids. Hungry for fame, money, and drugs. I set up these installations with them. Bodies on bodies: naked, half-dressed, on display and for sale. This is art you can take home and fuck, do with it what you will. I pawn them off to the software tycoons and the virtual CEOs and new money and newer money, and seventeen-year-old fucking junior Ivy League pranksters who've got more money than they know what to do with, and they spend on me, and I love it. I'm a pop star. I'm a bad girl. I'm on every damn screen. Everybody wants to talk to me. I have oxygen. It goes into me. I breathe. I am whole. The road to glamour is a dead end.

(Lizzie B exits bar.)

Excerpt from *Prodigal Kiss*

CARIDAD SVICH

MARCELA: There were five of us. A plumber, a factory worker, a mother, her child, and myself.

No one else. Only sea and sky.

We had food and water for two days. All we had for power was oars. We took turns rowing.

We would row for eight hours and stop.

If we were lucky, a current would catch us and we could rest our arms.

After two days, there was only a bit of water left—drinking water, that is—

and we hadn't spotted a plane or fishing boat anywhere that could save us.

So we bobbed in the waves, tired of rowing, and watched the sharks swim past.

We started praying.

The child fed on his mother's dry tit, and the plumber screamed.

He screamed of fire, snow, and of a head full of shit. He screamed so much he couldn't get a word out.

After a while, his eyes became fixed. Like glass.

He was staring. At nothing. But he was still alive.

The factory worker grabbed the child and began to strangle it with his large hands.

The mother looked at him with a half-bent smile, and offered the factory worker her tit to suck.

The plumber kept staring.
I looked at the sky.

It was of a deep, penetrating blue. And as it grew dark,
I thought I could see five moons lit up at different points in the
sky, creating a path of light.
And I thought of my Santiago, and how it would shine at
night—
  (Half-sung:) *"Me voy pa Santiago. Pa Santiago me voy . . ."*
The sky turned black. For an instant. And the boat swayed.
I looked up again at the sky.
I looked for a plane that would see us and not take aim, as we
kept bobbing in the waves.
But there was nothing. Only sky.

And I began to cast my eyes down,
As the factory worker tied the mother's mouth with kisses,
while the child hung between them like a doll grown limp and
forgotten.
The plumber stared, and kept staring. His eyes were now fixed
on my suitcase.
I could feel the plywood and ropes tying this mess of a boat give
out under the weight of the sea.
And that's when he fell, the staring man, straight into the water,
straight down.
And we all looked up. For a moment. Catching our breath as
the wind spit on the breeze.

The factory worker let go of the mother, and started cursing
"Coño carajo mierda. Coño carajo. Coño carajo."
The mother looked at me.
She clutched my arm, digging her nails into my skin, the dead
child between us.
I couldn't move. I couldn't think.
I could only look up. And keep looking.
And just as my eyes were beginning to burn

178

from the heat of the sun and the sting of the air,
I saw a plane. A small plane flying out from under some wrecking clouds.
And I waved with my free arm, and yelled with my harsh throat.
And then we all started waving. Like featherless birds.
Waving and yelling with our mouths dry as rags, and our brains drunk from the sun
"Bread. Ice. Santiago . . . "
The plane touched close. Hot metal.
And slowly it lifted us up into the chill of the air.
And we trembled. And held our breath.
And kissed, kissed all that was alive in us.

And it was then that I felt I could really look straight ahead without fear of what would find me,
For I was safe in the belly of that plane. And I knew earth's will had been done.
Whatever else would come to me, I would no longer be at the water's torturous mercy.

Excerpt from *Waterless Place*

C. DENBY SWANSON

GRACE, late thirties, the niece and caretaker of an old woman who has recently attempted suicide, finally opens up to her long-lost cousin, Walter, a lay minister.

GRACE: I went to Wal-Mart that afternoon. I made a point of yelling across the living room, Dottie do you need anything? As much to fool ourselves as anyone. I said, I'm going to pick up a few things, do you want something? And the idea was, when I got back she'd be gone.

And she got close this time. Close.

I called the ambulance, because that's what we'd planned. The truth is, I didn't even know what she'd done yet. I walked in the kitchen and picked up the phone, I didn't even look. I called, and then I went to her room.

She had lived for twenty-five years on half the organs most people require. This time, they weren't failing her quite fast enough. Despite what she had done to herself, I was five minutes too early.

The ambulance arrived, and it turned out she wasn't close enough. Doctors at Presbyterian Hospital stuck a needle into her neck and from there a tube into her body and with that tube they pumped out three bottles of pills and the effects of a sharp razor, they pumped in saline and antibiotics and twelve pints of blood. They pumped back in the nerve damage and the blindness and the colostomy and the heart condition and whatever was eating away her capacity for good, honest breath, she's got them pumping all of that back into her, all that life. It was a river. She wakes up again feeling this torrential river inside of her, and realizes there's no river in Heaven, she's not in Heaven, she's still on the other side, and maybe she'll never get across now, maybe God is getting her back for even daring her own end, that's the river she feels, that's the river she's in.

The psychologist asked me if I helped her and asked me if I knew, and the doctor said, I save lives, that's what I do, that's what I do well.

I am not a violent woman. But I lunged for him. I used both hands. I hauled him into Dottie's room, I pulled his face really close to her body. I managed to hold him there, underwater, for a brief moment, and I said WHAT DO YOU SMELL? I may have been screaming. WHAT DO YOU SMELL? He said, I smell smoke. I said, Yes. That's right.

She smoked until she decided to die. I always found that funny, the one thing that might actually kill her.

So when you say you prayed for her at the hospital that night, I wonder what you prayed for.

I prayed so often that I am at a loss for what to do with myself now. I prayed every day. I breathed in prayer. I counted my change at the grocery store in prayer. I filled up my car, I pumped prayer into my gas tank. I prayed that she would go quickly. Somehow. Shit, even Christ died and was buried. He suffered and then he died. Today they'd hook Him up to a machine and He'd lie there like a vegetable, doctors would have brought Him back, no chance to rise again after three days, no it would have been thirty years in that kind of wilderness, three hundred years, three thousand years, Revelation happens and the tribes of Israel open the seventh seal, it's empty and they wonder, Our messiah is supposed to come back, where is he? A hospital bed, the constant sound of beeping in His ear, an oxygen machine, a visit from the Blessed Virgin once a week but He is unable to feel her squeeze His hand. God forbid she roll away the stone herself. I was trying to roll away the stone for Dottie and instead I rolled it in front.

But you visited her in the hospital and she died in her sleep five hours later. What did you say?

He walks through waterless places seeking rest, but he finds none. Matthew 12:43.

The verse says that this man rids himself of an evil spirit and returns eventually to the house that he left, only to find it empty. He doesn't fill it with anything positive or long-lasting and he winds up worse off than he was before.

When I came back from Wal-Mart the house felt empty, like it was expecting her to be dead, but then, I don't know, maybe it got lonely seeing all that blood without its body so it held on to her and now I have too. She opened up her neck to let all this illness out and let pure oxygen in and it should have been over. But the pillowcases had held her head, and now I can't let them go. I thought at first I'd have to burn them, a testament of some wicked story, Lord knows I couldn't have them cleaned, someone would think I'd killed her. So I could start with the pillowcases, but what else. Everything has blood on it. Everything smells like smoke. Even I do, now. The books, the mementos, the curtains, the rug. It all soaked her in.

I was sitting here. I heard an inhale when they say she went, an echoing raspy inhale. She smoked for forty years and the particles collected on her lungs and that's where I was sitting when she finally went. I found myself sitting in her lungs, with all her stuff around me, attached.

The Old Rugged Cross

STACI SWEDEEN

An African-American woman speaks.

I don't want you to think I'm stuck up or nothing. I mean, when the rest of you all are carrying on, and you all sounding so serious and intelligent, my mind is carrying on in another direction entirely. My mind is so far to the left of the page that I'm all the way over in that margin where the little hole is. I'm writing on an entirely different page. 'Cause almost everything is funny to me. I can't help it. Even things that shouldn't be. Like funerals.

This good friend of mine died recently, and it was sad. Real sad and all.

Me and this other friend did the whole black clothes thing, don't even get me started on that, why sadness and blackness got all stirred in together. Even if it does have that slimming effect. So the whole church is packed, and we're sitting there in this pew and pretty much right at the top of the service this old lady got up to sing. This lady was older than dirt, honey, and she stands up there and starts right in on "The Old Rugged Cross." I immediately start thinking that she was probably living when Christ was doing his thing, you know, and her old lady voice is warbling on like this—

(Imitating) "And the oooooold ruugggged crossssss." She's just slipping and sledding down every note in the whole hymnal, and she was bad! Really bad! It just cracked me up. I start doing everything I can to keep from laughing out loud—holding my hand over my mouth, pinching myself, tears are streaming down my face, I'm thinking if she doesn't shut up pretty soon I'm gonna have to fling her to that hill far away, dear Jesus, plus my friend that died really loved music, so I got this vision

of him rising out of the coffin and saying "What did I ever do to you all to deserve this?!!" The friend that I was with is getting really pissed off at me. As if this was something I could help! My shoulders are shaking and then my friend's shoulders start shaking, pretty soon we are both peeing in our pants, making that snorty noise like we've entered pig heaven, and baby—once that image was in my mind—there was no turning back. Finally the two of us were asked to leave the service. I mean, we were asked to leave! My friend was so beside himself that he had to exit down the aisle on his hands and knees. He's still not talking to me.

I tried to explain how my mind works but all he would say was, "It was blasphemous to carry on like that at a Baptist service." But it was funny. Honestly, it *was* funny. And I know better now.

(Pause)

'Cause it was wrong.

Excerpt from *South of Adams, West of Figueroa*

MAYA WASHINGTON

Los Angeles, California. KENNEDY DANIELS *is an African American woman in her twenties moving through the death of her father.*

KENNEDY: I didn't know how to deal, so I went inside myself and I did everything not to reach out. Not to feel or experience life or loss because it just hurt so much. I didn't want anyone to see me lose it. I did though, inside Bloomingdale's. It's so embarrassing. I can't even go there to this day. That week before the funeral, Mom was such a mess. I don't know if you remember, but she had me get the burial clothes. Everything. The suit, the socks . . . underwear—all of it. So, I called in a favor from Mark, he was working on a soap opera at the time. He put me in touch with this suit designer. We had lunch at CPK, I looked at a few sketches and I felt fine, like happy I was able to do this for Daddy. Then after lunch, I went to Bloomingdale's to buy him some boxers, a T-shirt, and socks and . . . I never realized that T-shirts . . . white cotton ones anyway, all come in packages of like two and three. And I thought, I only need one of each. Thank God I finally found a nice Polo undershirt on a hanger by itself. All of a sudden the most eerie and horrible feeling came over me. I realized that I was holding the last T-shirt he'd ever wear. And I just freaked out. I freaked out. I was just bawling my eyes out, trying to suck it in so I wouldn't make so much noise. But it was loud and awful. Absolutely horrible. I was so embarrassed. That just made it worse. Then, all the sudden there's this crowd of like ten people, a security guard and this fragrance girl from Estée Lauder are hovering over me. I just wanted to disappear like the little white ashes on the tip of a burning cigarette. Just flake off and blow away. I don't even remember how I got home that night. Ever since then, I've prayed for more time. There's just not enough time in this life to be with the people we love. It's like every day, every hour comes and goes so quickly. I hate knowing that each day is a day closer to death. I don't like it. Days turn into years and then it's over. And it's only a series of memories that fade with time. First it was the smell of his skin. Or the smell of his freshly pressed white cotton shirts . . . I mean, it's all fading—even the sound of his laugh. I'm starting to forget his voice—that deep baritone voice that melted all my nightmares away, like steaming lava just flowing until my fears would transform. He helped me see them for what they were, pathetic little black coals trying to interfere with my peace. I miss him. It's been two years, Eden. And I miss him. With every breath I miss him.

Excerpt from *A Candle for the Blessed Virgin*

EILEEN WILLIAMS

GUADALUPE is a scrappy Latina, high-school dropout, homeless. She sells candles outside a large Catholic cathedral in a Southwest border town.

She has been eavesdropping on the confession of a man in his late teens to a young priest. They've left the church and Lupe is crowing to herself.

GUADALUPE (*Furtively emerging from a confessional booth*): I'm home free. He doesn't know if he's gay but he's afraid he's finding out while having so many great times at the rectory?

Your problem is growing, Father Pepé. How long can you veil this? You're lucky this one isn't actually a boy anymore, Father. I know how *you* sympathize with him but I don't think contemplation of Our Lady will change his situation. You and I both know he's been worshipping at the hem of your robe for a reason. I've seen the altar boys when they come over and have popcorn, watch movies, and dance around your living room to loud music, but what about *my* problem, Father?

I'm living in your cathedral. I've gotten used to my little confessional booth, Father; I see things and hear things. But how long until that nosy janitor sweeps behind the statue in the chapel and finds my stuff? I can't carry my clothes all day on the streets.

They're gonna be your streets, too, Father. They're calling you, because your secrets are my secrets. After mass, people leave you alone in Our Lady's house, I see your good-byes to the good townspeople, Father. You're not waving, but drowning, honey.

And nobody knows but me.

So far.

The cathedral's not your haven anymore, it's mine. It's my security blanket against the cold nights and the colder parishioners. Too many of them are starting to notice me. I'm not really anonymous anymore, am I, Father? They point and stare at *me*, Father . . .

What will they do to *you*?

Sparkles in the Rear View from *The Ghost Moments*

RANDY WYATT

BETHANY is a young woman in her twenties with a pair of sunglasses in her hands. She sits in a chair.

BETHANY: Aunt Diane used to take me to swimming practice in her rusted-out 1971 Impala. Sometimes I would sit in the front seat, the hot vinyl sticking to the parts of me that weren't covered by my Wonder Woman one-piece swimsuit. It was my favorite time of week—not the swimming, I hated that, the other girls all screaming and splashing each other for an eternal hour, by the end of which I was desperately longing to see the slim woman with the brown-tinted sunglasses appear near the exit, striding in to come claim me. No, it was the drive—there and back. It was our time each week. She would say "I've never had a niece before, so tell me if I'm doing things right" as we'd pull up to the ice cream shack after practice. She was a seventies goddess, a Charlie's Angel—Farrah had nothing on her. I'd messily devour a huge brownie sundae but always keep one fascinated eyeball on her, sipping her can of Tab with just that one calorie, reading some tan-colored paperback, absently brushing her feathered bangs out of her face. I was in awe of her, I wanted to be her. I loved sitting next to her, chatting with her as if I too was a young independent seventies jet-set woman instead of a dumpy nine-year-old girl going to swimming practice. We'd listen to "Hot Child in the City" on the radio and turn it up so loud I thought my mother would pop out of the dashboard and scream at us to turn it down, but she never did, and that was cool. Sometimes Diane would flatten out the back seat and I would sunbathe as we roared down the highway,

189

blasted by the hot cross-breezes flowing through the four open windows. Once I had a sniffle, and my mother had insisted on me bringing, not a package, but an entire box of tissues. I discovered that if I pulled out one after another, the mad breezes would turn the yellow tissues into golden faeries, skittering, flying all about, butterflies in a cyclone, all around me. And though my mother would have told me "stop wasting Kleenex," Diane just laughed and accelerated just a little more, so that the car soon was a magical cavern, a private grotto for Diane and the faeries and me.

She had a small prism, like a marble, that hung on fishing line from her rear view. Sometimes, I would stare at it when I sat in front, and think that I was hypnotized, and watch it break the afternoon sunlight into little spectrums, splashed all over the car interior. I wanted to scoop up these miniature rainbows and put them in my pocket, to somehow capture the magic of being older, sophisticated, independent, mysterious, that feeling that being with Aunt Diane gave me.

I tried to tell Mother but she never really understood. "Honestly," she'd say, waiting for a saucepan of margarine to melt, "I don't know when Diane is going to grow up and get a nice guy for herself. Settle down." But I didn't want Aunt Diane to "settle down." "Settling down," to me, meant being still, meant the fun was over and you had to come in and get ready for bed and "settle down." And if that's what Mother meant, then I didn't want Diane to settle down ever, ever, ever. At night I would dream of road-tripping with her, just the two of us, lounging on beaches, sipping iced teas, reading novels or racing cars just ahead of Burt Reynolds and Dom DeLuise, winning by a nose.

I never told Mother about Kevin, not out of deceit, but because I never really thought to. Once Kevin appeared, he showed up more and more at our ice cream shacks and pizza nights out. At first, I didn't want him along, but Diane knew how to have a boyfriend and a niece at the same time. Sometimes she would light up her Virginia Slim and with the smoke curling around her catlike eyes she'd tell him "Go along now. The girls need their time together." And he would ruffle my hair, peck Diane on the cheek and go. And then we would instantly turn to each other and talk about him. "Do you think he's cute?" "Is he always that goofy in restaurants?" and on we'd go, laughing and laughing. Soon, he was that wacky neighbor you didn't mind, and even kind of liked. At the time, I had no idea he was black.

Sometimes, now, if I concentrate, I remember what it was like to be truly color blind, how to look at someone and not break them into categories, like some cheap robotic analysis. Once you go past that point of knowing why the glances turned suspicious, awkward, uncomfortable, when your mother tells you she's taking you to swimming lessons from now on and you realize that you know why, once you learn the subtle art of intolerance through being polite, through Bible verses and better judgment, through safety by disassociation, all you want to do is go back and unlearn it all. You want the tissues to turn back into faeries, and rainbows to explode over your car, and race on and on with your Aunt Diane forever.

I wear the sunglasses she gave me the last time I saw her. I wear them whenever I want to feel older, sophisticated, independent, mysterious. Because of her, I know how. Because of her, I know a lot of things. Rock on, hot child.

Bull's-Eye from *The Ghost Moments*

RANDY WYATT

THERESE, a young wheelchair-bound woman, wheels herself onstage. During this speech, she mimes stringing a bow, retrieving an arrow, and notching it into her bow, facing the audience.

THERESE: Ever since I became a "cripple," people think it's my legs I miss the most. Nope. It's the respect.

During the first year, I didn't talk to anyone. Before I found Eddie. He was hanging on the wall of a sports equipment shop, one that took me a half-hour just to get up the stairs to get into. I knew it was love from the first second I saw him. I plucked him off the wall and I knew it was destiny, baby, him and me. I told the cashier that I was taking up archery. "Good for you," she told me.

For months, all I did every day was take Eddie out back and shoot cans. Arrow after arrow after arrow. I'd shoot a can off the stump from ten yards, and my mother on the porch would cry out, "Good for you, honey."

She bought me a target, which I looked at for a very long time. "That's the 'bull's-eye," my mother said, as if I didn't know, as if I were six years old, like the wheelchair had taken me back through time or something. "That's what you aim for."

Close up, the red spot in the middle seems so large. I know at larger distances it becomes a challenge, but to me, there was another target inside that red spot—a bull's-eye within that bull's-eye. When I set it up, it was that inner bull's-eye I was aiming for. Dead center of the dead center. I started hitting it. Over and over.

I signed up for competitions. "Good for you," they told me. I started winning competitions, one by one. All of them. Juniors, divisional, regional. Nationals. And people stopped telling me how good it was for me. They started being very quiet. Which was exactly what I had been aiming for all along.

This morning, I qualified for the Summer Olympic Games. Archery is one of the few sports that you can qualify for even if you started training later in life. Or early in your second life, depending. Every so often, when I mention it to a waiter or a bystander, someone tells me "Good for you." But they don't understand.

(She starts drawing her bow back.)

To me, good was never, never the aim. I now live my life on getting closer and closer to God. When I get there, I'll have a few questions. From now on, it's never good for me. It's absolutely

(She lets it go.)

perfect.

Contributors

Janet Allard's plays include *Incognito* (Guthrie Theater commission), *Loyal* (Guthrie and The Children's Theatre Company joint commission), *The Unknown: a silent musical* (Jonathan Larson Fellowship), and *Untold Crimes of Insomniacs* (developed in the Playwrights' Center's PlayLabs, a Guthrie/University of Minnesota BFA program 2004 Guthrie Lab premiere). Producing theaters include Mixed Blood, the Kennedy Center, Playwrights Horizons, Yale Rep, the Yale Cabaret, Access Theater in New York City, and theaters in Ireland, England, Greece, and New Zealand. Janet has received two Jerome Fellowships at the Playwrights' Center, where she is a core member. She holds an MFA from the Yale School of Drama.

Margaret Baldwin has produced her plays and solo and ensemble works throughout the United States. She first performed *Deepest Part of the Creek* with jazz artists at the Montana Artists Refuge (2003). *The Wet Nurse Sings* was produced by Synchronicity Performance Group (Atlanta) in *Anton Acts Out* (2002) and as part of *Red Curtain Cabaret* in Helena, Montana (2003). *Her Little House* received a 2004 AT&T Onstage Award for its world premiere at Horizon Theatre Company (Atlanta). Margaret has an MFA from the Iowa Playwrights Workshop and is a member of the Dramatists Guild.

Trista Baldwin's plays include *Patty Red Pants, Electropuss, Sex and Other Collisions, Chicks with Dicks I*, and *Chicks with Dicks II: Battle with Cannibal Sluts in Outer Space!* Trista's work has been produced and developed in New York City, Los Angeles, Austin (Texas), Bloomington (Indiana), Portland (Oregon), Seattle, Phoenix, and Australia by groups such as the Empty Space Theatre, Circle X, Stark Raving, HERE, Urban Stages, Hypothetical, La MaMa ETC, Overlap, and New Georges. She is the recipient of 2004 and 2005 Jerome Fellowships at the Playwrights' Center.

Abi Basch is a 2004–2005 and 2005–2006 Jerome Fellow at the Playwrights' Center. Her play *Voices Underwater* was in the Bay Area Playwrights Festival and Theater Emory's Brave New Works Series and was a finalist for the Weissberger Award at Williamstown Theatre Festival. She works closely with Physical Plant Theater in Austin, Texas, and is a core member of Austin Script Works. In 2005 she will receive an MFA in playwriting from the University of Texas.

Paul D. Bawek, a member of Actors' Equity Association, has an MFA in acting from the University of California–Davis and an MFA in directing from Southern Illinois University–Carbondale. His produced works include *No Fault* and *The Cabin* (WSIU TV), *CrossRoads* and *Falsies* (the Studio Theatre), *Gold Country Tales* and *Twain Tales* (the Fantasy Theatre). He is a winner of the Parkland Short Plays Contest, the Paradise Players One-Act Competition, and an Archie Award for best new play (SIU–Carbondale). His published works include *Change, First Kiss,* and *Undercurrents,* Volume III and IV. Paul teaches theater at Florida Southern College.

Anne Bertram's plays include *Liability* (2002 Tennesee Williams One-Act Prize winner), *St. Luke's* (1999 Studio Z commission, 2001 premiere, Theatre Unbound in Minneapolis), *The Donner Gold* (2000 Playwrights' Center Jones Commission), and *Sherry's Basement* (2003 premiere, Theatre Unbound). She is managing director of Theatre Unbound and an associate member of the Playwrights' Center.

William Borden's plays have won thirty-five national playwriting competitions and have had more than two hundred productions. The film version of his play *The Last Prostitute* was shown on Lifetime Television in Europe and is available on video. His novel, *Superstoe,* was recently republished by Orloff Press. A core alumnus of the Playwrights' Center, he is a member of PEN; the Dramatists Guild; the American Society of Composers, Authors, and Publishers; and the Authors Guild.

Carlyle Brown's plays include *The African Company Presents Richard III, The Little Tommy Parker Celebrated Colored Minstrel Show, The Negro of Peter the Great,* and others. "White Girl from the Projects" was developed in PlayLabs and premiered at the Pillsbury House Theatre as part of Carlyle's *Talking Masks,* coproduced by Carlyle Brown and Company, 2004. His commissions include Arena Stage, Houston Grand Opera, The Children's Theatre Company, Alabama

Shakespeare Festival, and Actors Theatre of Louisville, which cocommissioned *Pure Confidence*. Carlyle has received fellowships from the New York Foundation for the Arts, the Minnesota State Arts Board, the Rockefeller Foundation, the National Endowment for the Arts, Theatre Communications Group, the Pew Charitable Trust, and the McKnight and Jerome Foundations through the Playwrights' Center, where he is a core alumnus. He is also an alumnus of New Dramatists. Carlyle is currently on the board of directors of Theatre Communications Group.

Cory Busse is a playwright and humorist in Minneapolis. His play *Little Vines* was a semifinalist for the Playwrights' Center's 2003 PlayLabs Festival. In addition to plays and screenplays, Cory has written for *A Prairie Home Companion*, Salon.com, and PBS' *Mental Engineering*.

Sheila Callaghan's plays *Kate Crackernuts, Scab, We Are Not These Hands, The Hunger Waltz, The Catherine Calamity, Dead City*, and *Crawl Fade to White* have been produced or developed with the Playwrights' Center, ASK Theatre Projects, Playwright's Horizons, Soho Rep, Actors Theatre of Louisville, New Georges, Annex Theatre, LAByrinth, the Flea, and elsewhere. Her awards include the Princess Grace Award, a Chesley Prize for Lesbian Playwriting, a MacDowell Fellowship, a Playwrights' Center Jerome Fellowship, and commissions from EST/Sloan Foundation and South Coast Repertory.

Joan Calof is a playwright and performance artist. She received a Jones Commission from the Playwrights' Center, where she was twice selected as an associate member. She has published in several journals including *Rag Mag* and in an anthology of scenes for mature actors titled *A Grand Entrance* (Dramatic Publishing). She has performed her monologues at many venues, including the Minnesota History Center, the Playwrights' Center, and four fringe festivals, to favorable reviews.

John Carter is a former merchant seaman living and writing in Maryland. His credits include poetry and fiction in numerous publications and several dozen industrial film scripts. He has acted on stage and screen and has presented his poetry with or without music in nightspots, on radio, and on television. A revue of his poetry and lyrics appeared in New York.

Erica Christ is a published playwright and short story writer. She is the founder and artistic director of Minneapolis-based Cheap Theatre. Over the last seventeen years her plays have had many productions in the United States and Canada. Erica is a core alumnus of the Playwrights' Center.

Beth Cleary's *Findings Uncertain: A Play about Adoption in Three Pieces* was included in the June 2003 Theatre Unbound Festival of New Play Readings at Boston Theatreworks. The play received its first reading at the Playwrights' Center, as did her other short plays, *Break* and *Dialectical Soup. Break* was published in the fall 2003 issue of *Cross-Cultural Poetics.* She directs and teaches theater at Macalester College in St. Paul, Minnesota.

Bill Corbett's plays include *The Big Slam, Hate Mail* (cowritten with Kira Obolensky), *Heckler,* and *Ridiculous Dreaming,* an adaptation of Heinrich Boll's *The Clown.* He recently wrote *The Stuff of Dreams,* a Guthrie Theater touring production. His plays have been produced by Primary Stages (New York), Woolly Mammoth (Washington, D.C.), A Contemporary Theater (Seattle), and many other theaters. He was also a writer and performer for TV's *Mystery Science Theater 3000.*

Jeannine Coulombe has written several full-length plays, which have been produced in Minnesota and Iowa. Her play *The Vacant Lot* won the National AIDS Fund CFDA-Vogue Initiative Award for Playwriting from the Kennedy Center in 2001. She is an artistic associate with Theatre Unbound (Minneapolis). She has been a member of the Playwrights' Center since 1997. She received an MFA from the Playwrights Workshop at the University of Iowa in 2003.

Stephen R. Culp is the author of *The 13 Hallucinations of Julio Rivera, Life on Pluto, The Fool Jumps, Let's All Clap, Decadent Lawyers in Heat, Gods in Relief, Kitty,* and *The End of the World and Every Day After.* His work has been produced at the Magic Theatre in San Francisco, the Lark Theater in New York, Manhattan Class Company, and the Organic Theater in Chicago, among others. He happily boasts that he's a descendant of Mark Twain, and he's a member of the Dramatists Guild.

Lisa D'Amour is a playwright and multidisciplinary performance artist who lives in Brooklyn, New York. She is a core member of the Playwrights' Center, where she has received a Jerome Fellowship and two McKnight Advancement Grants, and a member of New Dramatists.

Vincent Delaney's plays include *The Robeson Tape, The War Party, MLK and the FBI,* and *Kuwait.* His plays have been seen at the Humana Festival of New Plays, the Alabama Shakespeare Festival, Woolly Mammoth, the Empty Space Theatre, A Contemporary Theatre, the Illusion Theatre, and the Cleveland Play House. Vince is a core member and 2004–2005 McKnight Advancement Grant recipient at the Playwrights' Center, and a former Bush Foundation Artist Fellow. He holds an MFA in playwriting from the University of California–Davis.

Matt Di Cintio is a playwright, translator, and freelance dramaturg. His productions include a translation of Wilde's *Salome* (PlayMakers Repertory, 2003), an adaptation of *Moby-Dick* (University of Richmond, 2003), *Nosegays on Monday* (Glasslight, 2003), and *The Valets* (Outward Spiral/Minnesota Fringe Festival, 2004), with dramaturgy at PlayMakers Rep, the Guthrie Theater, TheatreVirginia, and the University of Richmond. He holds an MA in romance languages from the University of North Carolina and BAs in theater and French from the University of Richmond. He has received W. M. Keck grants for playwriting and translation.

Paul Dios' writing has been featured in award-winning magazines such as *The Manhattan Review, Escritoire*, and *Release*. His plays have been produced and/or workshopped at the John Houseman Studio Theatre for its New and Emerging Works Festival; La MaMa ETC; the Atrium Theatre; Playwrights Horizons; 13th Street Repertory; and most recently, Perseverance Theatre (Alaska). He is currently serving as artistic apprentice at Theatre de la Jeune Lune in Minneapolis.

Stephanie Fleischmann has received grants, fellowships, or residencies from New Dramatists, the National Endowment for the Arts Opera/Music Theater, the New York Foundation for the Arts, the MacDowell Colony, Hedgebrook, Mabou Mines/Suite, the Tennessee Williams fellowship program, and Sewanee. Her plays include *Red Fly/Blue Bottle, Viper, The Street of Useful Things, The Hotel Carter* (Frederick Loewe Award), *Eloise & Ray* (Whitfield Cook Prize, *Village Voice* Season Highlight), *What the Moon Saw, The World Speed Carnival*, and *Far Sea Pharisee*. Her work has been produced and/or developed at HERE, Act II Playhouse, New Theater, the Lincoln Center Theater Director's Lab, Roadworks, Interart, New Georges, Soho Rep, the Public, the Knitting Factory, the Hangar, and Voice & Vision.

Diane Glancy is a professor at Macalester College in St. Paul, Minnesota. She has published two collections of plays, *American Gypsy* and *War Cries*. Among her productions are *Jump Kiss*, in Native Voices at the Autry in Los Angeles (2002); *Lesser Wars*, Voice & Vision Theater Company in New York (1999); and *The Woman Who Was a Red Deer Dressed for the Deer Dance* and *The Women Who Loved House Trailers*, Raw Space, Sage Theater Company in New York (1998–1999).

Carolyn Goelzer is a writer and performer based in the Twin Cities. Her performance works include *Princess Power, Peas, Vicarious Thrills*, and *The Plant Society* and have been presented at the Walker Art Center, the Southern Theater, Red Eye, and Intermedia Arts. She has received awards from the Playwrights' Center and the McKnight Foundation, the Jerome/Dayton-Hudson Foundation, and the Minnesota State Arts Board. She is a core alumnus of the Playwrights' Center.

Bashore Halow is a 2003 and 2004 receipient of the Lark Theatre Company's Playwrights Week Residency Award for his plays *I'm Breathing the Water Now* and *Mean Streak*. Among his numerous New York City productions, *Cooper Savage* was produced by the Emerging Artists Theatre Company in 2002. He recently had a play read at the National Arts Club. Some of his one-act plays have been published by the One Act Play Depot.

Jordan Harrison's plays have been produced and developed at Actors Theatre of Louisville, Perishable Theatre, the Empty Space Theatre, Playwrights Horizons, and Clubbed Thumb. He is the recipient of the Heideman Award, two Jerome Fellowships from the Playwrights' Center, and a Lucille Lortel Fellowship. He is currently working on a commission from The Children's Theatre Company and the Guthrie Theater. Jordan coedits the annual *Play: A Journal of Plays*.

Jeffrey Hatcher's plays have been produced on Broadway, Off-Broadway, and at numerous theaters in the United States and abroad. In addition to the American Theatre Critics Association Award and Philadelphia's Barrymore Award for Best New Play, he's received fellowships and awards from the Playwrights' Center's McKnight and Jerome programs, the Charles MacArthur Foundation, the National Endowment for the Arts, Theatre Communications Group, and the Lila Wallace-Readers' Digest Fund. He is a member of the Dramatists Guild and the Writers Guild of America as well as a Playwrights' Center core alumnus and a New Dramatists alumnus.

Cory Hinkle is a playwright and actor from Bartlesville, Oklahoma. He received his BFA in performance from the University of Oklahoma. He is the recipient of a 2003–2004 Jerome Fellowship at the Playwrights' Center as well as a new play commission from the Guthrie Theater. His plays include *Unrequited Pop, The Magazine Girl, Across the Desert, Sex and Cigarettes,* and *Kid Dreams.* He has been a runner-up for the Princess Grace Award and a semifinalist for PlayLabs.

Eugenia Jensen is a core member of the Playwrights' Center and lives in St. Paul, Minnesota. Her plays *Grandmother's House, The Day Before the Day After, Welcome Home, Daddy,* and *Exit Interview* have been seen in theaters in Minnesota, New York, Maine, and California. She is currently at work on her first screenplay.

Carson Kreitzer's plays include *The Love Song of J. Robert Oppenheimer, Slither, Self Defense or death of some salesmen,* and *Take My Breath Away,* among others. She is a member of the Dramatists Guild and an associate member of the Playwrights' Center. She has received grants from the New York Foundation for the Arts, the New York State Council on the Arts, the National Endowment for the Arts, Theatre Communications Group, and two Jerome Fellowships and a McKnight Advancement Grant through the Playwrights' Center. She currently lives in Austin, Texas.

Jennifer Maisel's plays include *The Last Seder, Eden, Dark Hours, Mad Love, . . . And the Two Romeos,* and *Mallbaby,* which was developed at the Playwrights' Center's PlayLabs and ASK Theatre Projects. Her plays have been workshopped and produced in New York, Chicago, Washington, D.C., Minneapolis, San Francisco, and Los Angeles. Awards include the Roger L. Stevens Award (*Mad Love*), the Charlotte Woolard award for most promising new writer, and the Fund for New American Plays award from the Kennedy Center (*The Last Seder*). In addition, she was a winner of the California Playwrights Competition (*Eden*) and a finalist for the PEN West Literary Award (*Mad Love*) and the Heideman Award (*How I Learned to Spell*).

Melanie Marnich is the author of *Tallgrass Gothic, Blur, Quake, Beautiful Again,* and *The Sparrow Project.* Her plays have been produced by the Guthrie Theater, Actors Theatre of Louisville, the Dallas Theatre Center, Manhattan Theatre Club, American Theater Company, and the Playwrights' Center with Hidden Theatre. Her awards include two Jerome Fellowships and two McKnight Advancement Grants from the Playwrights' Center and two Samuel Goldwyn awards. She lives in Minneapolis and is a core member of the Playwrights' Center.

Allison Moore is a displaced Texan living in Minneapolis, where she is a two-time Jerome Fellow and former McKnight Advancement Grant recipient at the Playwrights' Center. Her plays include *Eighteen, Urgent Fury, CowTown, Hazard County,* and *The Strange Misadventures of Patty.* . . . She has received commissions from the Guthrie Theater, Eye of the Storm, and Actors Theatre of Louisville; and her work has been developed or produced at the O'Neill Playwrights Conference, Kitchen Dog Theater, InterAct Theatre Company, Madison Rep, Centenary Stage Company, the Jungle Theater, the Playwright's Center, and the Humana Festival. Allison is a graduate of Southern Methodist University and holds an MFA from the Iowa Playwrights Workshop.

Kira Obolensky's play *Quick Silver* (developed in PlayLabs and coproduced by 3Legged Race and the Playwrights' Center) was named most outstanding piece of experimental theater by Twin Cities critics in 2003. Her other plays include *Lobster Alice* (Kesselring Prize; finalist for Susan Smith Blackburn; published in *Best Plays by American Women 2000*; and produced in Minneapolis, Atlanta, California, Texas, and Off-Broadway) and *The Adventures of Herculina* (Honorable Mention Kesselring Prize, Edith Oliver Award, produced in Chicago and Minneapolis). Kira's new work includes *All Is Well in the Kingdom of Nice* (produced at Geva Theatre Center), *Hiding in the Open* (produced at the Great American History Theatre), and *A New House,* or *21 Lies for Four Characters.* She has received support from the Guggenheim Fellowship, the Bush Fellowship, and the Playwrights' Center Jerome Fellowship and is a current recipient of a Playwrights' Center McKnight Advancement Grant.

Dominic Orlando was a 2003–2004 Jerome Fellow at the Playwrights' Center, where he completed *Juan Gelion Dances for The Sun,* which was featured in the 2004 Bay Area Playwrights Festival in San Francisco. The play was developed at the MacDowell Colony in New Hampshire, the Edward Albee Foundation in Montauk, New York, and No-Pants Theatre through a grant from the New York City Department of Cultural Affairs. Dominic has also received commissions and fellowships from the Guthrie Theater, the Nautilus Music Theater (St. Paul, Minnesota), Bristol Valley Theater (Naples, New York), the Cornucopia Arts Center (Lanesboro, Minnesota), and a second fellowship to the MacDowell Colony.

Jeany Park's play *Falling Flowers,* about the Korean "comfort women," was first produced by Theater Mu in January 2002 and will receive its third production in the spring of 2005. Jeany has cowritten several plays with MaMa mOsAiC (Minneapolis). She is an associate member of the Playwrights' Center, where she also serves on the board of directors.

Stacey Parshall, a mixed-blood playwright and fiction writer, has had her plays developed at WordBRIDGE and read at the National Black Theatre Festival and in the Jungle Theater's Play Reading Series. She is also a playwright and dramaturg for the Pillsbury House Theater's Chicago Avenue Project. She is a recipient of two Playwrights' Center Many Voices Residencies and is completing an MFA in creative writing at Hamline University.

Erik Patterson's plays include *Tonseisha*; *The Making of Mary Kelly*; *Yellow Flesh/Alabaster Rose*, which won the Backstage West Garland Award and was a finalist for the 2004 PEN USA Literary Award; and *Red Light, Green Light*. His work has been workshopped and produced by Theatre of NOTE, the Evidence Room, the Actors' Gang, and the Lark Play Development Center. He is a graduate of Occidental College and the British American Drama Academy.

Mary Jo Pehl has been a contributor to NPR's *All Things Considered* and *The Savvy Traveler* on Public Radio International. She is a former writer and actor on *Mystery Science Theater 3000* on the Sci-Fi Channel. Her work has appeared in *Life's a Stitch: The Best of Contemporary Women's Humor*, the *Minneapolis Star Tribune*, and the *Minnesota Women's Press*. Her book, *I Lived with My Parents and Other Tales of Terror*, was published in 2004.

Elaine Romero's plays have appeared at Actors Theatre of Louisville, the Women's Project and Productions, Arizona Theatre Company, and the Working Theatre, among others. She has been a guest artist at South Coast Repertory and the Mark Taper Forum. The Pew Foundation and the National Endowment for the Arts have supported her award-winning plays, which have been published by Samuel French, Vintage Books, Smith and Kraus, and UA Press. She participated in the Sundance Playwrights' Retreat at the Ucross Foundation.

Mark Rosenwinkel is a core member of the Playwrights' Center, where he has received a Jerome Fellowship. His plays have had productions, readings, and workshops with theaters around the country, including the Idaho Shakespeare Festival and the Asolo Theatre (Sarasota, Florida). His four-person adaptation of *Moby-Dick* has been published by

Dramatic Publishing, and his most recent play, *Sanctus*, won the 2002 Writers' Digest Literary Award in the play script category.

Ellena Antoinette (Tina) Schoop studied and performed Senegalese dances from Africa. She recently participated in a performance workshop with Djola Branner and a workshop community performance with Chuck Davis' African American Dance Ensemble at the Ordway Center for the Performing Arts (Minneapolis). Ellena participated in the Twin Cities 2003 Fringe Festival. She was a 2003–2004 Playwright's Center Many Voices Resident.

Gwendolyn Schwinke's plays have been produced by Red Eye Collaboration and Cheap Theatre in Minneapolis and read at the Playwrights' Center and the Cherry Lane Theatre in New York. A monologue from her play *Thrown by Angels* is included in Heinemann's *Even More Monologues for Women by Women* (2001). Gwendolyn is a core member of the Playwrights' Center and a past recipient of the center's Jones Commission.

Buffy Sedlachek is a resident artist with Stages Theatre Company and literary manager of the Jungle Theater. A core alumnus of the Playwrights' Center, she has been awarded Minnesota State Arts Board Fellowships, Playwrights' Center McKnight Advancement Grants and Jones Commissions, a Jerome Foundation Travel and Study Grant, and a Theatre Communications Group Observership. Nominated three times for the Susan Smith Blackburn Prize for distinguished women playwrights, she is also the coauthor of two curriculum guides for teaching playwriting.

Amy Seham is a tenured professor at Gustavus Adolphus College in St. Peter, Minnesota, where she directs and teaches acting, directing, and playwriting. Her plays have been produced at the Minnesota Fringe Festival, the Perry Street Theatre, Shakespeare and Company, and Performance Studio Theatre in New Haven, Connecticut, where she was artistic director. Her book, *Whose Improv Is It Anyway?* (University Press of Mississippi, 2001), traces the history of improv comedy in Chicago.

Rosanna Staffa's work has been seen at the Mark Taper Forum's Taper, Too and the Odyssey Theatre Company in Los Angeles, Soho Rep and Off-Broadway in New York, and the Theatre Garage and the Playwrights' Center in Minneapolis. She has received new play commissions from the Guthrie Theater and the Children's Theatre Company. She is the recipient of an AT&T OnStage Award as well as a McKnight Advancement Grant and a Jerome Fellowship at the Playwrights' Center, where she is a core member.

Saviana Stanescu is an award-winning Romanian-born writer (*The Inflatable Apocalypse*, Best Romanian Play of the Year, 1999; *Final Countdown*, Antoine Vitez Center Award, Paris). Her texts have been presented and published in the United States, the United Kingdom, France, Austria, Germany, Hungary, Montenegro, Macedonia, and Romania. Productions in New York include *Yokasta* at La MaMa ETC Theater and *Waxing West* at the Lark Theatre. She has an MA in performance studies and an MFA in dramatic writing from New York University's Tisch School of the Arts.

Dane Stauffer studied at the Children's Theatre Company (Minneapolis) and graduated from New York University's Tisch School of the Arts. In addition to a three-year stint improvising and writing at Dudley Riggs' Brave New Workshop, he's had a dozen plays produced in the Twin Cities at the Jungle, Illusion, and Cricket Theaters, and in Tampa, San Diego, and the Edinburgh Fringe. He was featured on KTCA/PBS' Emmy award-winning *American Scream*.

Caridad Svich is a playwright, songwriter, translator, and editor. Her awards include a Harvard University Radcliffe Institute for Advanced Study fellowship and a Theatre Communications Group/Pew National Theatre Artist Grant. Recent premieres include *Iphigenia . . . a rave fable* at 7 Stages (Atlanta) and her multimedia collaboration with Todd Cerveris and Nick Philippou, *The Booth Variations,* in New York. She is editor of *Trans-global Readings: Crossing Theatrical Boundaries* (MUP/ Palgrave, 2004). She holds an MFA from University of California–San Diego and is a resident playwright of New Dramatists.

C. Denby Swanson is a graduate of Smith College, the National Theatre Institute, and the Michener Center for Writers at the University of Texas–Austin. Her work has been developed at the Women Playwrights Project, the Estro-Genius Festival, the Playwrights' Center's PlayLabs 2002, and the Southern Playwrights Festival; produced by Salvage Vanguard, the Drilling Company, and 15 Head; and published by Heinemann, Smith and Kraus, and Playscripts. She was a Playwrights' Center Jerome Fellow and McKnight Advancement Grant recipient, a William Inge Playwright in Residence, and is currently the artistic director of Austin Script Works.

Staci Swedeen is an award-winning playwright and professional actress. Her plays have been performed across the country, published in numerous anthologies, and presented in many festivals. A New York State Council for the Arts New Play grant recipient, a Lark Theatre Fellow, and a Dramatists Guild Fellow, Staci was commissioned by the Ensemble Studio Theatre/Sloan Foundation. She is a member of the Writers Guild of America and the Dramatists Guild. For more information, visit *www.staciswedeen.com*.

Maya Washington is an actress, choreographer, writer, and arts educator who lives in Minneapolis. A touring production of her one-act *Colorful Women of Invention* was produced at Youth Performance Company in 2003. *South of Adams, West of Figueroa* is her first full-length play. She received her BA in theater from the University of Southern California. Currently, she attends Hamline University's MFA writing program in St. Paul, Minnesota.

Eileen Williams holds a master's degree in English and an MFA in theater from the University of Iowa. Her writing has been published in the United States and England. After a career as an arts writer and editor, she currently is a director at a Twin Cities nonprofit organization.

Randy Wyatt is an award-winning playwright, director, and improv coach. His plays include *The Face of the Earth* (a finalist in Christians in Theatre Arts 1999 playwriting competition), *Anticipating Miles* (in the 2004 Columbus GLBT Theatre Festival), and *32 Awkward Silences* (in the 2003 Austin Script Works Out of Ink Festival), *Saturday Morning Forever*, and *Sonata Blue*. He lives in Grand Rapids, Michigan; Minneapolis, Minnesota, or Austin, Texas; depending on where his current project is located.

Performance Rights

Janet Allard, c/o Doug Rand at Playscripts, Inc., P.O. Box 237060, New York, NY 10023; ph.: 866-639-7529 ext. 82; fax: 866-639-7529; drand@playscripts.com.

Margaret Baldwin, c/o Heinemann.

Trista Baldwin, c/o Heinemann.

Abi Basch, c/o The Playwrights' Center, 2301 Franklin Ave. East, Minneapolis, MN 55406.

Paul Bawek, c/o Heinemann.

Anne Bertram, c/o Heinemann.

William Borden, c/o Heinemann.

Carlyle Brown, c/o Heinemann.

Cory Busse, c/o Heinemann.

Sheila Callaghan, c/o Heinemann.

Joan Calof c/o Heinemann.

John Carter, c/o Heinemann.

Erica Christ, c/o Heinemann.

Beth Cleary, c/o Heinemann.

Bill Corbett, c/o Carl Graham at Graham Agency, 311 West 43rd St., New York, NY 10036; grahamacnyc@aol.com.

Jeannine Coulombe, c/o Heinemann.

Stephen R. Culp, c/o Bruce Ostler at Bret Adams Ltd., 448 W. 44th St., New York, NY 10036; ph: 212-765-5630; fax: 212-265-2212; bostler.bal@verizon.net.

Lisa D'Amour, c/o Val Day at William Morris Agency, 1325 Avenue of the Americas, New York, NY 10019; ph: 212-903-1550; pfasst@wma.com.

Vincent Delaney, c/o Heinemann.

Matt Di Cintio, c/o Heinemann.

Paul Dios, c/o Heinemann.

Stephanie Fleischmann, c/o Heinemann.

Diane Glancy, c/o Heinemann.

Carolyn Goelzer, c/o Heinemann.
Bashore Halow, c/o One Act Play Depot, Box 335, Spiritwood, SK, Canada S0J 2M0; ph: 775-249-8151; plays@oneactplays.net.
Jordan Harrison, c/o Val Day at William Morris Agency, 1325 Avenue of the Americas, New York, NY 10019; ph: 212-903-1550; pfasst@wma.com.
Jeffrey Hatcher, c/o William Morris Agency, 1325 Avenue of the Americas, New York, NY 10019; ph: 212-903-1125.
Cory Hinkle, c/o Heinemann.
Eugenia Jensen, c/o Heinemann.
Carson Kreitzer, c/o cskreitzer@earthlink.net or c/o Judy Boals, Inc., 208 W. 30th St. #401, New York, NY 10001; ph: 212-868-0924; fax: 212-868-1052; jboals@earthlink.net.
Jennifer Maisel, c/o Susan Schulman, Agent, 454 West 44th St., New York, NY 10036; ph: 212-713-1633; fax: 212-581-8830; schulman@aol.com.
Melanie Marnich, c/o Bruce Ostler at Bret Adams Ltd., 448 W. 44th St., New York, NY 10036; ph: 212-765-5630; fax: 212-265-2212; bostler.bal@verizon.net.
Allison Moore, c/o Maura Teitelbaum, Abrams Artist Agency, 275 7th Ave., 26th Floor, New York, NY 10001; ph: 646-486-4600; fax: 646-486-0100; maura.teitelbaum@abramsart.com.
Kira Obolensky, c/o Patrick Herold at ICM, 40 W. 57th St. 16th Floor, New York, NY 10019; ph: 212-556-5600; pherold@icmtalent.com.
Dominic Orlando, c/o Heinemann.
Jeany Park, c/o Heinemann.
Stacey Parshall, c/o Heinemann.
Erik Patterson, c/o Heinemann.
Mary Jo Pehl, c/o Heinemann.
Elaine Romero, c/o Mark Subias at Mark Christian Subias Agency, 331 W. 57th St. #462, New York, NY 10019; ph: 212-445-1091; marksubias@earthlink.net.
Mark Rosenwinkel, c/o Heinemann.
Ellena Antoinette Schoop, c/o Heinemann.
Gwendolyn Schwinke, c/o Heinemann.
Buffy Sedlachek, c/o Heinemann.
Amy Seham, c/o Heinemann.
Rosanna Staffa, c/o Susan Gurman, The Susan Gurman Agency, LLC., 865 West End Avenue, Suite 15A, New York, NY 10025; ph: 212-749-4618.
Saviana Stanescu, c/o Marta Praeger, Robert A. Freedman Dramatic Agency, 1501 Broadway, Suite 2310, New York, NY 10036; ph: 212-840-5760.
Dane Stauffer, c/o Heinemann.
Caridad Svich, c/o New Dramatists, 424 West 44th St., New York, NY 10036; ph: 212-886-1814 or 212-757-6960; fax: 212-265-4738; newdramatists@newdramatists.org.
C. Denby Swanson, c/o Maura Teitelbaum, Abrams Artist Agency, 275 7th Ave., 26th Floor, New York, NY 10001; ph: 646-486-4600; fax: 646-486-0100; maura.teitelbaum@abramsart.com.
Staci Swedeen, c/o Elaine Devlin, Literary, Inc., 20 West 23rd St. 3rd Floor, New York, NY 10010; ph: 212-206-8160; fax: 212-206-8168; edevlin@aol.com.
Maya Washington, c/o Heinemann.
Eileen Williams c/o Heinemann.
Randy Wyatt, c/o the author at thecove@gmail.com or www.lostinthecove.com.